RANGE WARS

SOUTHWEST LIFE AND LETTERS

A series designed to publish outstanding new fiction and nonfiction about Texas and the American Southwest and to present classic works of the region in handsome new editions.

General Editors: Suzanne Comer, Southern Methodist University Press; Tom Pilkington, Tarleton State University.

Range Wars

Heated Debates, Sober
Reflections, and Other
Assessments of Texas
Writing *Edited by Craig
Clifford and Tom Pilkington*

SOUTHWEST LIFE AND LETTERS

SOUTHERN METHODIST UNIVERSITY PRESS

First edition, 1989
Requests for permission to reproduce material from this work should be sent to:
    Permissions
    Southern Methodist University Press
    Box 415
    Dallas, Texas 75275

Library of Congress Cataloging-in-Publication Data
Range wars.

    (Southwest life and letters)
    Includes index.
    1. American literature—Texas—History and
criticism.   2. Texas—Intellectual life.   3. Texas
in literature.   I. Clifford, Craig Edward, 1951–
II. Pilkington, Tom.   III. Series.
PS266.T4R36   1988   810'.9'9764   88-42632
ISBN 0-87074-282-5
ISBN 0-87074-273-6 (pbk.)

Illustrations by Charles Shaw

CONTENTS

The best American fiction has always been regional. The ascendancy passed roughly from New England to the Midwest to the South; it has passed to and stayed longest wherever there has been a shared past, a sense of alikeness, and the possibility of reading a small history in a universal light.

—Flannery O'Connor, "The Regional Writer"

If we could develop a taste for literary controversy we might someday even develop a literature. The literary life in Texas is as polite as Sunday school—and about as passionless. Surely a passion for letters ought to engender the same things other passions engender: malice, jealousy, wit, attacks, insult.

—Larry McMurtry, *The Texas Observer,* 26 February 1971

PREFACE

The main title of this volume, *Range Wars,* perhaps suggests that Texas literature in recent years has been a battleground for territorial conflicts among the state's writers. If so, that is exactly what we intend to suggest. Few would dispute the claim that the Texas literary scene over the last decade or so has been alive with controversy. This controversy has helped immensely to sharpen and to define the issues and questions concerning Texas writing that beg to be resolved—though, to be sure, it has supplied no irrefutable answers.

Such issues and questions exist in abundance: *Is* there a Texas literature? Assuming there is, what can be said about its aesthetic quality? How should Texas writers deal with the state's frontier past and urban present? What has been the impact of non-native writers on Texas letters? Has that impact been mainly good or mainly bad? What should be the function of the Texas Institute of Letters in promoting Texas writing— or should there even be a Texas Institute of Letters? What is—or should be—the role of women and minority writers in Texas literature? The list of questions that have sparked debate among Texas writers, critics, and interested bystanders over the last few years is a lengthy one indeed.

At the most fundamental level there are some who dispute the very notion of a "Texas literature." These people, if they are writers, usually want to be known simply as writers who, by chance, were born in Texas or now live in the state. They do not wish to be stigmatized by the label "regional writer." They argue that to separate Texas writing from the larger category of American writing is to "ghettoize" and trivialize Texas literature; it is to imply that Texas writers are judged by lesser standards than are employed to evaluate American writers generally.

If this is in fact the case, then any division of American literature—some of them necessary divisions, it would seem, given the enormous quantity of American writing—must create the same effect. Does the fact that critics normally categorize certain books as Southern or Western American literature or as American women's literature or as black literature ghettoize and trivialize such works? There may be a grain of truth in the argument of those who would answer yes to this question, but such subcategories seem to us desirable, even unavoidable, taking into account the vastness and variety of the whole of American literature. We begin, at any rate, with the premise that there is such a thing as Texas literature, and this collection is, therefore, addressed to those who care about that literature.

Since this is a book about literary controversy, there are no doubt those who will object to its essentially contentious nature. Why not try to douse the flames of contention among Texas writers, they may well ask, rather than risk provoking further controversy? It is a question that is raised to some extent even in the pages that follow. We are more than happy to grant the importance of cultivating literary friendships. Friendships among writers can be supportive, even inspirational. Historically this proposition has proved especially true for Texas writers who, if they have remained in the state, have often found themselves isolated in an environment indifferent, or even hostile, to art and artists. In such a situation the support of like-minded friends and colleagues is crucial, not just to the success of one's work, but to maintaining one's sanity.

Unfortunately, however, the downside of literary friendship is that it can all too easily degenerate into literary cronyism—into the kind of good-old-boyism that has for far too long dominated the "criticism" of Texas letters. Sad to say, while the climate for criticism in the state has improved somewhat over the last decade, we still have too much of the kind of mutual back scratching that Larry McMurtry described in 1981, in "Ever a Bridegroom." "Literary comradeship," McMurtry wrote, "is a fine thing up to the point at which it begins to produce a pompous, self-congratulatory, and self-protective literary culture." In Texas, he continued, cronyism "has produced exactly that: a pond full of self-satisfied frogs."

We do not wish to discourage friendships among Texas writers, but one of our basic convictions is that contention among writers can be an essentially healthy sign, else we would not have bothered to bring together these essays. It can help to dissipate some of that complacency and self-satisfaction of which McMurtry spoke. Certainly controversies have a way of transforming themselves into feuds, and some feuds among Texas writers have sprouted in recent years. Where there is debate, there can also be personal animosity. On the whole, however, literary contentiousness seems to us to indicate that most of the state's writers and critics have begun to take the idea of a Texas literature more seriously than they ever did in the past.

When writers and critics attempt more, set their goals higher, care more, they fight more—and, if history provides any precedent, they fight not just about abstracted literary quality, but about such things as the nature of a uniquely American literature, the Southernness of Southern Agrarians,

the characteristics of an Irish "national literature." In the
middle of the nineteenth century Emerson, in "The American
Scholar," chided the timid and called the brave to their literary
arms to produce an American literary and cultural identity.
The Southern Renaissance involved dead serious infighting,
as well as a rejection of Yankee ways. The Irish fought over
the "Irishness" of their literary renaissance with Celtic ferocity.

In his 1981 essay McMurtry, as part of his denunciation of
literary complacency in Texas, memorably depicted literary
criticism in the state as two writers getting into a fistfight in
a bar. McMurtry's piece has provoked a fistfight here and
there, no doubt, but it has also stimulated some earnest thinking and writing on Texas literature, some rip-roaring, high-
spirited name-calling, and other forms of controversy that
have given substance to the concept of a Texas literature and,
we think, to a new seriousness among writers who identify
with that literature.

We have seen, surely, some inconsequential posturing,
even dueling, in the wars that have heated up in 1980s Texas
literary life. Regional literary politics, without question, can
lead writers away from their art. But their art is never that
pure anyway—we can all agree there are no Texas Henry
Jameses around, thank God, and only a few who are trying to
be—and sometimes regional literary politics gives to writers
just the kind of pride and chip-on-the-shoulder contentiousness that they need to conceive of themselves as committed
artists. The recent political and egoistic literary haggling in
Texas may well assist the literature of our province, by means
of the growth of the very idea of a "Texas literature," to achieve
a maturity it has not previously displayed.

The essays that follow offer a variety of responses to
contemporary Texas writing—from iconoclastic pronouncements to literary folks flat whooping it up to some temperate
and relatively gentle reflections. The only common characteristic of the essays is that the authors all make it refreshingly

clear that Texas literature matters to them; and, furthermore, that it matters which Texas literature is good and which is not. Let it be made plain, right off, that these are not detached, academic exercises in literary criticism. Critical analysis without love and hate, we contend, defeats its own purpose. Perhaps H. L. Mencken's position that criticism is simply prejudice made plausible is a bit extreme, but if the prejudices allow the literature to shine forth in all its glory or shameful inadequacy, then let the prejudices fly.

In a sense, the essays brought together here are historical documents. They trace not so much the history of Texas literature over the past few years as Texas writers' and critics' evolving perceptions of that literature. Most of them began life as articles or speeches that addressed some hotly debated topics relating to Texas writers and writing.

A. C. Greene's list of "The Fifty Best Texas Books," first published in the August 1981 issue of *Texas Monthly,* was by the author's own admission subjective, but also daring. It attempted to discriminate and judge, something not many critics of Texas writing had been willing to do prior to the 1980s. Greene apparently accomplished his goal: he provoked. The purpose of Larry McMurtry's now famous essay, "Ever a Bridegroom: Reflections on the Failure of Texas Literature," was, in part at least, to dispute Greene's contention that fifty good Texas books exist. When it appeared in the *Texas Observer* in October of 1981, the public response was immediate and sometimes explosive. The essay was the first firecracker on the string; it ignited the series of squabbles that have enlivened the Texas literary scene in the 1980s.

Three of the pieces included between these covers were intended, in one way or another, as responses to "Ever a Bridegroom." Craig Clifford fired off "Horseman, Hang On," which appeared in the *Observer* a few months after McMurtry's essay. It defended the importance—and continuing vitality—of the "cowboy myth" in Texas literature and culture, a myth

McMurtry had pronounced damaging to the efforts of Texas writers. José E. Limón, in "A 'Southern Renaissance' for Texas Letters," wholeheartedly agreed with McMurtry's dim view of the quality of Texas writing—at least the writing produced by Anglo Texans. Limón proclaimed that the real flowering of Texas literature will begin in South Texas with the impressive work of a growing band of Texas Mexican authors. Clay Reynolds decided to survey the state's literary quarrels, including the McMurtry essay and its aftermath, from the perspective of an author who had just published a first novel and found himself, somewhat unexpectedly, being branded a "Texas writer." He called the result "What Does It Take to Be a Texas Writer?"

Other voices got into the fray as well. In "Requiem for a Texas Lady," Celia Morris, a "radicalized Texas woman," flung some well-aimed stones at the largely masculine Texas mythos. Meanwhile, Don Graham was mounting an old-time Texan assault on the Texas Institute of Letters. In his satirical broadside, "Palefaces vs. Redskins: A Literary Skirmish," he charged that the TIL kowtows to writers who have immigrated to Texas from other regions—particularly the East. In "Arbiters of Texas Literary Taste," James Ward Lee, with tongue lodged firmly in cheek, traced the line of succession of writers, past and present, who have either willingly accepted or actively campaigned for the position of Texas's literary "potentate."

But enough is enough, decided Marshall Terry. He took issue with the idea that writers should take issue with one another. In "The Republic of Texas Letters," Terry, taking on the role of peacemaker in these literary range wars, defended the TIL and spoke out in favor of literary "fellowship" among the state's writers. And, finally, Tom Pilkington figured out how to round up all of these stray points of view and get them to market. His "Herding Words: Texas Literature as Trail Drive" offers a broad overview of some of the issues relating to Texas literature and an assessment of that literature from the perspective of the larger body of American literature.

Here they are, then, a collection of highly spirited and highly opinionated essays about Texas writing, sure to prove stimulating and maybe even eye-opening for readers with an interest in contemporary Texas books and writers.

Craig Clifford
Tom Pilkington
Stephenville, Texas

RANGE WARS

THE FIFTY BEST TEXAS BOOKS

A. C. Greene

These are my choices for the fifty best Texas books. I would like to emphasize that these are the best books *about* Texas. By that I mean Texas is their main subject or, in the case of fiction and biography, their chief setting. They are not the best books written by Texas authors (in fact, not all the authors are Texans), and they may not be the most important Texas books—but don't let's get off into a thicket of objections and explanations: the quality of the books speaks for itself.

I hope I will not sound too arbitrary with bold assertions: "This is my pick . . . My choice is . . . This is the best." But I feel there hasn't been enough of this in Texas letters. I think Texas has needed more positive criticism, more outspokenness from within, with regard to its own culture. The bold international braggart when it comes to material trivia, Texas has an inferiority complex about its art. Behind that mask of bigness, Texas can't believe it has the ability to bring forth, in and of itself, something worthy of mankind's recognition.

Texas has relied too long and too completely on the opinions of outsiders.

The book from which this article is excerpted (to be published by Pressworks Publishing in Dallas) includes descriptions—like the twelve used here—of each of my selections. The books are not listed in order of preference or ranked in any other way. I have not attempted to pick something from each form of literature, but I haven't slighted any type of writing, either, unless you might say that I excluded textbooks and technical manuals. But frankly, if I had been attracted to a book of that sort, I would not have hesitated to include it as well.

So I boldly submit my choices for Texas's fifty best books. And whether you are outraged or in agreement, I give you leave to make your own.

•*CORONADO'S CHILDREN,* J. Frank Dobie. This book is the one that made it possible for a Texas writer to stay home and make a living. When *Coronado's Children* was published in 1930 (in Texas), it was picked up by the Literary Guild—the first non-Eastern publication ever chosen by the Guild or Book-of-the-Month—and became a national success. The book created Frank Dobie's Mr. Texas image, and it stayed with him for the rest of his life. Although the Guild payment was a pittance by today's standards (and his Texas publisher went bankrupt before he received his full royalties), the consequences were more valuable than dollars. First off, Dobie got a Guggenheim grant, which enabled him to do *Tongues of the Monte,* but more important, he could now sell anything about Texas he wanted to write, and this opened the field for others, too.

Coronado's Children is folklore about lost mines and buried treasure, caves full of gold bars, and jack-loads of Spanish silver. (How many of us had heard of a jack-load before we read Dobie?) I know of no other Texas book from which so many writers have filched so much.

When I met Frank Dobie some twenty-five years after

first reading *Coronado's Children,* I told him it was still my favorite of his books. He acted hurt. I think friends had convinced him that his more serious works, like *The Longhorns* or *The Mustangs,* better fit his literary stature. Or maybe it was Mrs. Dobie. After his death, when I was living on his ranch on a Dobie-Paisano Fellowship, she and I became friends, and I suspect Bertha wished he had been more of a footnote counter. Bless her gracious memory, I'm glad he wasn't.

•*BLESSED McGILL,* Edwin Shrake. Like so many authors, Edwin "Bud" Shrake started out as a newspaper sportswriter. In fact, when I went to work for the *Dallas Times Herald* in 1960, he, Blackie Sherrod, and Gary "Jap" Cartwright were on the same staff and were joined, or succeeded immediately, by Dan Jenkins and Steve Perkins—you talk about a golden age of sportswriting. But all that time Bud was writing novels, a good many of which seemed to be reaching for some truth about life (Texas life) that needed to be explained. *Blessed McGill* (1968) combines the best of Shrake's talents: an appreciation for the absurdities of existence, a recognition of irony's major role in the world, highly suggestive humor, and a decent amount of historical and anthropological research so that the book never spews off into the campy pseudo-historical "nonfiction" that characterizes a whole school of American prose. *Blessed McGill* is hilarious. It begins with Peter Hermano McGill's boyhood in Austin following the Civil War. He is reared by a devout (but a little cuckoo) Catholic mother, but through a series of circumstances he becomes as much a brother to the Indians as to the Anglos, enough that he is guarded by a renegade half-breed, a Karankawa throwback called Badthing. But Shrake does not sacrifice truth or wisdom for sheer entertainment, and when McGill—by a sequence of inevitabilities—moves toward sainthood in Taos, it is not merely an absurd plot twist but a subtle study of what spiritual deliverance really is.

•*JOURNAL OF THE SECESSION CONVENTION OF*

TEXAS, 1861, edited from the original by Ernest W. Winkler, state librarian. This is the most tragic document in Texas history—and the most dramatic. Officially and meticulously (469 pages, not one of them wasted), it details the enveloping tornado that swept even Texans with better sense into the catastrophe that history knows as "the Southern cause." Although the events in these official minutes are, without the slightest question, pushing pell-mell to disaster, we see the galleries full (literally) of cheering supporters as folly succeeds folly: the counting of votes, the naming of delegates, the resolutions, speeches, motions, letters, reports, braggadocio, brave and foolish acts, grandiose Confederate schemes. Why couldn't sanity have been allowed, just one day, or in one session, to rise above the malarkey, the empty rhetoric? Because at this point, in Texas, to have opposed secession would have meant total dishonor—as happened to Sam Houston—or even death. The *Journal of the Secession Convention* (1912) makes all this plain, without commentary. Its compressed chronology pushes it along like a brilliant historical novel. The Secession Convention (illegal in its inception) was called for January 1861, and by March 25, when it adjourned, Texas was committed to the cataclysm that destroyed, perhaps forever, the chances of these United States to be a happy nation.

• *INTERWOVEN,* Sallie Reynolds Matthews. A number of charming women wrote books, or portions of books, about their experiences in Texas: Mary Austin Holley, Jane Cazneau, Amelia Barr, Libby Custer, Melinda Rankin, to name a few. But Sallie Reynolds Matthews, in *Interwoven* (1936), gave us a lifetime view, not that of a visiting journalist or traveler. And what she wrote tells more about daily life on the frontier than any comparable narrative. Not only was Sallie bright but she caught and understood the eternal rhythms of society. Born in West Texas in 1861, she tells of girls and boys in love, of foolish but lovable brothers and (a few times) husbands, of weddings and babies—but never in a sentimental vein. This is a delightful book, written around the Reynolds and Matthews families, who intermarried and whose affairs were (and are) so bound together as to be inseparable, justifying the title. It is also the history of a large part of the cattle frontier from the 1860s to modern times. Without setting out to do so, Matthews shows us the differences between that Texas society and ours—which lifts *Interwoven* out of the family memoir class and makes it a historical tool.

• *UNCOVERED WAGON,* Hart Stilwell. You think all the old-time Texans worshiped their fathers and learned lessons of manliness and integrity from them? Not necessarily. *Uncovered Wagon* (1947) seems to be written around a core of autobiography, and Billy, the boy in the book, grows up hating and fearing his father, who is called only "the Old Man." Stilwell, who got pretty cranky as he aged, argued loudly and damningly with me when I suggested that the book was autobiographical, but you don't need an Eskimo to tell you there's ice in Alaska. (Stilwell was an unpredictable cuss, and once at a party where a friend and I were singing and playing hymns on a guitar and a harmonica, he proceeded to strip off his clothes and sit, stark naked, in the middle of the floor until we stopped. Then he talked.) *Uncovered Wagon* takes place in those uneasy years just before World War I, and Billy and the Old Man spend a lot of the book working in the fields and living unpleasantly along the back roads of Texas. But the circumstances of the story are secondary to the boy-man, son-father relationship. You don't find many Texas writers who can face the bitter reality of rural poverty in a changing society as Stilwell does, and this book is one of those rare Texas works that convinces the reader that it speaks for thousands of others—call it cynicism, or whatever. Some who knew Stilwell better than I did—and I didn't know him well at all—say his streak of frustration and cynicism kept him from being the great writer he should have been. I'm neutral, but *Uncovered Wagon* is evidence that Texas benefited when he did put his angry heart in it.

•*PALE HORSE, PALE RIDER,* Katherine Anne Porter. Some people say *Pale Horse, Pale Rider* (1939) is not a Texas book, but they forget, perhaps, that the volume of that title contains two other famous short novels, *Old Mortality* and *Noon Wine,* both with Texas settings. In any case, I don't care. I insist that *Pale Horse, Pale Rider* is the best Texas fiction ever written. The story takes place during World War I, but it is as contemporary as any feminist work since. Miranda, a newspaper reporter (who, as a young girl, also appears in *Old Mortality*), hasn't a taint of outdatedness; she is headstrong and independent, yet gentle and, despite herself, romantic. But none of this gentleness allows Miranda to be pushed around—except by a terror bigger than she is.

Katherine Anne Porter, the one time I met her, acidly denied that she had been a newspaper reporter in Dallas—or Texas. I have always thought it strange she was so bitter in her disavowal of things Texan but did so many of her best stories with a Texas background. (I once spent half a day trying to find her birthplace in Brown County.) Katherine Anne Porter told an interviewer, shortly after *Pale Horse, Pale Rider* was published, that she could not really imagine "creating" a story, that everything she had written or would write must be based firmly on a foundation of actual experience. Who knows?

•*I AND CLAUDIE,* Dillon Anderson. Until Clint Hightower (the "I") and his sidekick, Claudie, first appeared in *Atlantic Monthly,* to which I had recently been given a subscription as a graduation present, I had despaired of ever seeing Texas humor in such an august (then) journal. It was enough for me that *I and Claudie* (1951) was picaresque (haven't you always wanted to have a genuine occasion to use that word, after hearing it all the way from ninth grade through graduate school?), but in addition, it was Texas that Clint and Claudie roamed, conning their way, a pair of up-to-date Gentle Grafters outsmarting bankers and oilmen but almost as often falling victim to their own softheartedness or their own cleverness. Years later I discovered that Dillon Anderson was not some ink-stained wretch but a highly successful Houston corporate lawyer. I eventually met him at a Texas Institute of Letters dinner in Houston, but it was one of those "hello, I've always liked your work" kinds of meetings, and he died before I had the chance (or the nerve) to sit down with him and explain why I wished he had been a flop as a lawyer so he could have done nothing but write.

• *13 DAYS TO GLORY: THE SIEGE OF THE ALAMO,* Lon Tinkle. Lon Tinkle was the most courtly man of letters Texas has ever produced, but he had strange little fears. When Walter Lord's intensive study of the Battle of the Alamo, *A Time to Stand,* came out in 1961, I stated in a review that whereas Lord's work was more inclusive and historically evaluative than Tinkle's *13 Days to Glory* (1958), I preferred Lon's book because it was more revealing. While factually sound, it explored the mystery of what kept those men at the Alamo to die, as Lord pointed out, somewhat needlessly. I got a phone call that afternoon from Lon Tinkle expressing his gratitude, but also his wonder. Since we were, at that time, book critics on competing Dallas newspapers, he had quivered (his word) all week that I might seize the opportunity to elevate the fine Lord book and denounce that of my rival. (Those who recall his matchless diction can hear his voice on that sentence.) I was the one to quiver a few weeks later when I introduced Walter Lord at a book-and-author luncheon, but he made only an amused reference to the review as we parted: "Oh . . . that."

Tinkle's *13 Days to Glory* gives the essence of the Alamo story without attempting to exhaust history's explanation. He is fair to the Mexican attackers, even Santa Anna, and does not hallow the slain Texans; neither does he insist that all the legends are true. But he makes implicit the strange consensus of the defenders to stay and die—and that is what makes *13 Days to Glory* such uncommonly good reading.

• *SOUTHWEST,* John Houghton Allen. This collection of autobiographical essays about an older lifestyle on the border of South Texas defies description. John Houghton Allen writes with great sympathy for the people and the land where he lived, but he writes more like a nobleman than a rancher. The short pieces in *Southwest* (1952) are subtly tinged with that air of privilege, of being birth-appointed to a role in history that may have been tragic but was necessary. That's not the tone one expects to find in Texas ranch tales. His gentlemen ranchers and their spoiled sons are as devoted to horses as to wives—with the exception, now and then, of other men's wives. The Mexican ranch hands and their folklore go back to Spanish times, when privilege came naturally—an inheritance passed along by the Spanish ranchers who settled the kingdom of the Rio Grande in the eighteenth century to the dynastic Anglos who superseded them (or stole their titles and their privileges). But *Southwest* is a fascinating, unusual book about Texas that isn't duplicated by any other writer. Reading it is like reading abut a foreign country; Randado is akin to Brigadoon, and fantasy fits snugly within Allen's romantic style.

• *HOLD AUTUMN IN YOUR HAND,* George Sessions Perry. Perry was a good writer, and his best writings owe their power to the Texas society they describe. *Walls Rise Up* (1939) is an amusing novel about two down-and-out Texans trying to survive in the Brazos bottoms by doing as little work as possible. But I like *Hold Autumn in Your Hand* (1941) because it attempts more. *Walls Rise Up* is a trifle on the Texas trite side. *Hold Autumn in Your Hand* goes deep into the character and integrity of Sam Tucker, a Texas tenant farmer in those same bottoms, who, though "too poor to flag a gutwagon," continues to fight nature, the seasons, the river, and a good many of his fellow men for the satisfaction of bringing something (himself, if you want some philosophy) from the earth, despite never being able to pull back and watch. But it is something more than just another man's fight against nature; *Hold Autumn in Your Hand* is full of country humor—pretty racy, of course—and Texas common sense, presuming it's different from other kinds of common sense. We may have lost that old tie with the earth our immediate forefathers had, but modern readers will find that no barrier to enjoyment. Perry's later disabilities (crippling arthritis) and his unexplained death (his body was found in a Connecticut river two months after he apparently wandered away from his home) ended what was, at the time, the most successful Texas writing career to be found. (*Hold Autumn in Your Hand* was made into a film titled *The Southerner,* with native Texan Zachary Scott playing Sam Tucker.)

• *THE INHERITORS,* Philip Atlee. In 1940 there weren't many books being written about contemporary Texas, other than poor farmer or Depression novels, although by then Texas had turned a corner very few of its residents and almost none of its writers recognized: it had become an urban state. In 1968 I did detailed research at the University of Texas at Austin and found October 1928 to be the exact month when Texas swung to having more people living in cities and towns than on farms, ranches, or other rural locations. In *The Inheritors* Philip Atlee (James Phillips) wrote about the urban scene in Fort Worth. This isn't Cowtown. This is the young social set—carousing, driving big cars too fast, going from party to country club to any kind of devilment and eventual crackups—physical and mental. It's an overindulged generation. One scathing chapter has this lost tribe out on the Fort Worth dump at night shooting rats for thrills, they're so bored with the usual run of fornication, drunkenness, and bragging about

Daddy's money. The story is well done, and it was told thirty
or forty years before its time. Few Texas books have been able
to repeat the harsh dismay, the inspired brutality, of *The
Inheritors.*

•*HORSE TRADIN'*, Ben K. Green, D.V.M. That noblest
of all New York editors, Angus Cameron, called me in the
summer of 1965 and asked if I were kin to a Dr. Ben Green. I
said no, after briefly discounting the significance of the final *e*
on my name when it comes to claiming kin. Angus said I was
the loser, because Green had written a story ("Gray Mules")
in *Southwest Review* that was a classic. He suggested I call Ben,
which I did. This began a literary adventure I am not likely to
repeat, because there can be only one Ben Green in a lifetime.
Although I was closer to him than anyone in the book world, I
never uncovered the real Ben Green. I never tried. But I had a
unique triumph: he never got mad at me. Ben was a spell-
binder—he admitted, with charming haste, he knew more
about horses than any person alive (I believed it). He became,
on publication of *Horse Tradin'* (1967), a major writer—yet
most of his fellow writers would not admit it. Why? Because
he was also hardheaded, vain, perverse, dissembling, and im-
possibly cantankerous at times. For example, those D.V.M.
initials on *Horse Tradin'* never appeared on another Green
book, because they were false. He tried to hide the fact that he
had served time in Huntsville, that he had been married, and
that he was relatively young—at least ten years younger than
he looked. He was a glorious storyteller who got furious if
you implied his stories were fiction, yet his writing in things
like *The Shield Mares* proves his humanity was greater than he
could face. He loved my wife and he once sent a fellow 150
miles to plant a special peach tree he was giving her. When he
died, I cried. I couldn't help it.

My other thirty-eight choices for Texas's best books are:

A Ranchman's Recollections, Frank S. Hastings
Hound-Dog Man, Fred Gipson
The Evolution of a State, or, Recollections of Old Texas Days, Noah
    Smithwick, compiled by Nanna Smithwick Donaldson
*A Texas Ranger and Frontiersman: The Days of Buck Barry in
    Texas, 1845–1906,* edited by James K. Greer
Sam Bass, Wayne Gard
Horseman, Pass By, Larry McMurtry
Texas History Movies, text by John Rosenfield, Jr., illustrations
    by Jack Patton
The Bone Pickers, Al Dewlen
The Butterfield Overland Mail, Waterman L. Ormsby
Triggernometry, Eugene Cunningham
Charles Goodnight: Cowman and Plainsman, J. Evetts Haley
Adventures with a Texas Naturalist, Roy Bedichek
The Great Plains, Walter Prescott Webb
This Stubborn Soil, William A. Owens
The Wonderful Country, Tom Lea
A Journey through Texas, Frederick Law Olmsted
*Six-Guns and Saddle Leather: A Bibliography of Books and Pam-
    phlets on Western Outlaws and Gunmen,* Ramon Adams
The Mexican Side of the Texas Revolution, Carlos E. Castañeda
Love Is a Wild Assault, Elithe Hamilton Kirkland
Johnny Texas, Carol Hoff
The House of Breath, William Goyen
Blood and Money, Thomas Thompson
A Texas Trilogy, Preston Jones
Armadillo in the Grass, Shelby Hearon
The Comanche Barrier to South Plains Settlement, Rupert Norval
    Richardson

. . . And Other Dirty Stories, Larry L. King
The Gay Place, William Brammer
A Time and a Place, William Humphrey
I'll Die before I'll Run: The Story of the Great Feuds of Texas, C. L.
     Sonnichsen
Six Years with the Texas Rangers, James B. Gillett
Great River: The Rio Grande in North American History, Paul
     Horgan
Events and Celebrations, R. G. Vliet
Sironia, Texas, Madison Cooper
A Woman of the People, Benjamin Capps
The Raven: A Biography of Sam Houston, Marquis James
Leaving Cheyenne, Larry McMurtry
Adventures of a Ballad Hunter, John A. Lomax
Goodbye to a River, John Graves

EVER A BRIDEGROOM: REFLECTIONS ON THE FAILURE OF TEXAS LITERATURE

Larry McMurtry

About fourteen years ago, as I was trying to force several rather disparate essays to join hands and look like a book about Texas, I complicated the problem by adding an essay called "Southwestern Literature?"—emphasis on the question mark.

At the time the piece was thought to be harsh, not because I had questioned the existence of a Southwestern literature but because my attitude toward the Holy Oldtimers— Dobie, Webb, and Bedichek—was less than reverent. In fact, it wasn't much less than reverent: the books of all three men were given more in the way of praise than they really deserved. A recent attempt to retrace the literary steps that led me to that essay proved very rocky going indeed. Time has begun its merciless winnowing; today the sheaves these three men heaped up look considerably less substantial than they seemed only fourteen years ago.

J. Frank Dobie, by far the most prolific and most popular

"Ever a Bridegroom" was presented as a lecture at the Fort Worth Art Museum in September 1981; it was first published in the 23 October 1981 issue of the *Texas Observer.*

of the three, has fared much the worst. It is now clear how much his books needed the support of his forceful and infectious personality. Like Will Rogers and other raconteurs, he was better in person than on paper. Less than two decades after his death in 1964 a contemporary reader finds that Dobie's twenty-odd books are a congealed mass of virtually undifferentiated anecdotage: endlessly repetitious, thematically empty, structureless, and carelessly written.

His reputation has declined so swiftly that it was recently possible for the editor of the state's most popular magazine to refer to his writings as "bedtime stories for ten-year-olds." True, although the world he wrote about must now seem irrelevant to most ten-year-olds. Dobie had the energies of a Mencken, but not the reach. It is his energies and his application, rather than the literary result of them, that make him seem still worthy of salute.

In years to come Roy Bedichek's *Karánkaway Country* and *Adventures with a Texas Naturalist* are apt to give more pleasure to readers than all the books of his friend Dobie—merely because they are written well. I don't think Bedichek had much to say, but his eye and his whimsy were served by an excellent, flexible prose style. He is as appealing—if as minor— today as he ever was.

Nonetheless, I am not sure that the Bedichek influence has been wholly benign. The bucolic essay may be a sweet form, but it is also a limited one—indeed, almost a retrograde form, the most likely route of nostalgic retreat from our increasingly urban realities. I think we have too many bucolics, too many Richard Jeffrieses, W. H. Hudsons, Gilbert Whites. Now what we need is a Balzac, a Dickens, even a Dreiser. Texas writers have paid too much attention to nature, not enough to human nature, and they have been too ready to fall back on the bucolic memoir or country idyll rather than attempting novels, poems, and dramas. Minor forms only rarely prompt major books, and the lack we suffer from most is a lack of major books.

So far, by my count, we have a total of one.

Our literature is not *evenly* minor—some Texas books are better than others—but none of it is major.

Were I set the task of seeking an exception to that dictum, I would probably try and make a case for Walter Prescott Webb. Unfortunately, I think the case would fail. Webb's achievement was genuine, but small. He had a first-rate mind and he continued to extend its reach throughout his life, but the yield, finally, was two important books, *The Great Plains* and *The Great Frontier,* the latter being by far the more impressive. It is one of the few Texas books that bespeak a true intellectual vitality. By contrast *The Great Plains,* comprehensive though it is, seems dull and rather wooden. Webb lost much of his energy to academic storekeeping, and more of it to his huge romantic work on the Texas Rangers. Though he matured late, he matured fully, and might finally have delivered a masterpiece had he not been killed. The longer Webb wrote, the greater seemed his potential, an unusual thing. In writers late growth is not the norm, in Texas or not.

When I say that Texas has produced no major writers or major books, the exception I most expect to hear argued against me is Katherine Anne Porter. Again, I think the argument would fail, but hers is a subtle case and merits more prolonged address than I can give it here.

Alone among Texas writers of her generation, Miss Porter thought of herself as an artist and had the equipment to be one. Though often sharply critical of modernism, she touched most of the modernist bases, usually at a time when no one else was occupying them. A large part of her artistic equipment was dedication—or stubbornness, as she called it. Another part was what might be called a high neurosis, driving her from place to place and prompting her to leave, like dumped baggage, a remarkable body of evasions and misrepresentations, through which her biographers will be sorting for the next few decades.

In her *Paris Review* interview she speaks of the various other "half-talents" she possessed: for dancing, singing, acting. Reading through the *Collected Stories* now—Miss Porter being no longer around to distract one with her charming accounts of their composition (some of these are better stories than the stories)—one is forced to think that all but the best of her work—perhaps half a dozen stories—is, like her singing and dancing, the work of a half-talent.

Oh, the whole talent was there, and a fine talent it was: but a talent seldom either fully or generously put to use. Miss Porter believed in a pure style; hers, at times, is purified almost to the vanishing point. By her account, she did this in the name of an aesthetic, removing the local and the immediate in order to reach the timeless and universal.

Unfortunately for her aesthetic, and unfortunately too for many of her stories, the local and immediate is the true street of fiction—at least of the sort of realistic fiction she was trying to write. The great ones, the Dickenses and Balzacs, Flauberts and Hardys, Faulkners and Tolstoys, wasted none of their time attempting to boil the accents of their own times and places out of their fiction.

I doubt, though, that it was aesthetics that drove Miss Porter to smooth her sentences so carefully. More likely what was at work was her profound evasiveness, an uncertainty not so much about what she knew as about what she could bring herself to admit about what she knew. For all her trafficking with revolutionaries and mad poets, for all her scorn of middle-class convention, she was genteel to the core. It may be that all that purification of style was undertaken in order that she might conceal her own experience perfectly—perfectly meaning even from herself.

Within her terms she is very skillful, but her terms are seldom embracing, or even interesting. Too often she reminds one of a minor French *belles-lettrist*: an intense purity of style concealing a small—very small—grain of experience. Compare her stories to Chekhov's, or Flannery O'Connor's, and they seem fragile, powdery, and frequently just plain boring.

Of course, there are a handful of noble exceptions, when the artist won the battle with the lady. These few fine stories satisfy—despite the alabaster prose—because Miss Porter has for once not been able to hide her own fascination with—and terror of—such primal concerns as lust, revenge, birth and death. But these stories are few. In too many cases the story struggles against the all but opaque language, and loses; one very seldom feels that the experience has been allowed its full life.

Ironically—how often this happens to those who think they live solely by their fiction—Miss Porter's passionate, often vengeful essays now seem more alive and probably more permanent than all but a few of her stories. In attack she was always quite confident, and far less genteel.

In her own time Katherine Anne Porter virtually eluded criticism. The surface she presented, both in person and in her fiction, was taken to be impeccable, when in fact it was merely inscrutable. Edmund Wilson paid her a few compliments, chided her gently for irrelevance, and that was about it. Both as an artist and as a person she seems to have needed to attract attention, and yet to escape it, and in large measure she succeeded. Gertrude Stein, whom Miss Porter did not like, once made a famous remark about—I believe—Oakland, California. There was no there there, she said. I feel very much the same way about the fiction of Katherine Anne Porter. The plumage is beautiful, but plumage, after all, is only feathers.

Despite its criticism of the Holy Oldtimers, my fourteen-year-old essay seems on the whole a surprisingly optimistic document. It was written in the mid-sixties, when there was every reason to think that Texas was about to experience a literary coming of age. There were at least a dozen young writers loose in the state whose potential everyone was ready to welcome. *Goodbye to a River* had appeared, and *The Gay Place,* and *Adam's Footprint,* all interesting beginnings. A flowering seemed not merely imminent, it seemed already to have occurred.

One reason for my optimism was my sense that the country—or Western, or cowboy—myth had finally been worked through. It was clear by then that this myth had served its time, and lost its potency; insofar as it still functioned it was an inhibiting, rather than a creative, factor in our literary life. The death of the cowboy and the ending of the rural way of life had been lamented sufficiently, and there was really no more that needed to be said about it.

Moreover, this realization seemed widespread. Most of the young Texas writers I knew were quite willing to face the fact that they were city people; they all seemed well aware that the styles which would shape their lives and sustain their fiction were being formed in Houston and Dallas, not back on the homeplace, wherever it had been.

For reasons I don't fully understand, my mid-sixties optimism was unfounded, generally as regards our literary flowering, specifically as regards the Western myth. At a time when the latter should have ceased to have any pertinence at all, drugstore cowboyism became a minor national craze. Boots became trendy in New York just as the last of the real cowboys took to wearing dozer caps and other gear more suitable to the oil patch and the suburb.

I recognize now that in the sixties I generalized too casually from a personal position. *In a Narrow Grave* was my formal farewell to writing about the country. It had dominated four books, which seemed enough, and I began rather consciously to drain it from my work. I proceeded to write three novels set in Houston, one set in Hollywood, and—most recently—one set in Washington, D.C.

I didn't deplore country living—still don't—but I had no doubt at all that urban life offered me richer possibilities as a novelist. Granting certain grand but eccentric exceptions, virtually the whole of modern literature has been a city literature. From the time of Baudelaire and James, the dense, intricate social networks that cities create have stimulated artists and sustained them. No reason it should be any different in Texas, since we now have at least one or two cities which offer the competitions of manners upon which the modern novel feeds.

It was thus something of a shock, as I started looking at my shelves of Texas books in preparation for this essay, to discover how few of them deal with city life. Not only are there few readable city books, but many of the country books are filled with explicit anti-urbanism. Writer after writer strains to reaffirm his or her rural credentials.

Why? The vast majority of Texas writers have been urbanites for decades. Many are veterans not only of the Texas cities, but of the cities of the East Coast, the West Coast, and Europe.

Where has this experience gone? Where are the novels, stories, poems, and plays that ought to be using it? Why are there still cows to be milked and chickens to be fed in every other Texas book that comes along? When is enough going to be allowed to be enough?

Part of the trouble, I am afraid, lies with Texas readers, who, if my experience is any indication, remain actively hostile to the mere idea of urban fiction. Virtually every time I give a lecture in Texas I find myself being chided by someone in the audience because I have stopped writing "the kind of books I ought to write."

Evidently, in the eyes of these readers, only my first three books were the kind I ought to write—the ones that happened to deal with small towns and cowboys. *Leaving Cheyenne* forever is what my readers seem to want.

Speaking at the University of Texas a year or two ago, I was confronted by a young lady who suggested, in distinctly resentful tones, that my next book would probably be set in Princeton, which, in her innocence, she took to be synonymous with the East. When I pointed out that I was more familiar with Virginia than New Jersey, she said, "Oh well, all those places up there are so close together."

Her attitude, though severe, was not much different from that of many old friends, who sigh wistfully and cast fond glances at their copies of *Leaving Cheyenne* when they ask me what I'm writing now.

The readers' attitude, reduced to basics, is that the writer who doesn't want to keep rewriting the book that pleased them most is merely being selfish. Once a writer manages to write a book that gives a reader pleasure, his duty, presumably, is to repeat the book so that the reader may repeat the pleasure. Attempts to offer the reader more advanced and subtle pleasures—or, indeed, pleasures that are in any way *different*—are not only unnecessary, they are unwelcome.

This is an understandable prejudice, but one which any healthy writer will ignore.

Unfortunately, not enough Texas writers are ignoring it. Too many of them love repeating themselves—after all, it's easier than thinking up something new to say. Many seem to find offering up an endless stream of what might be called Country-and-Western literature an agreeable way to make a living. Easier to write about the homefolks, the old folks, cowboys, or the small town than to deal with the more immediate and frequently less simplistic experience of city life.

What this amounts to is intellectual laziness. Most Texas writers only know one trick, and seem determined to keep from learning another. The result is a limited, shallow, self-repetitious literature which has so far failed completely to do justice to the complexities of life in the state.

The Dallas critic A. C. Greene is plainly aware of many of these problems. In the April issue of the *Lone Star Review* he comments forcefully and perceptively on the very anti-urbanism I have been describing. A few months later, in *Texas Monthly,* he published a list of his fifty favorite Texas books which, in my view, merely confirms the tenacity of the bias he himself has criticized.

He was kind enough to list two of my books in his selection, and they were *Horseman, Pass By* and *Leaving Cheyenne,* the first two. It seems incredible to me that a critic as intelligent as Mr. Greene could choose a piece of juvenilia such as *Horseman, Pass By* over, say, *Terms of Endearment,* unless a) he hadn't read the latter, or b) he was approaching the material from a position of deep bias.

The deep bias is the more likely explanation. I think this bias operates against all Texas writers who deviate from whatever typecasting they may have acquired. In the same essay Mr. Greene prefers Edwin Shrake's *Blessed McGill*—a Western book—to the same author's *Strange Peaches,* a city book. Within the minuscule context of our local literary life, *Blessed McGill*—like *Leaving Cheyenne*—is overpraised, *Strange Peaches* completely neglected. Not much time has passed since the two books were written, but the little that has has been kinder to the latter than to the former. *Blessed McGill* is an interesting tour de force that seemed to work when it was published—our *Sot-Weed Factor,* as it were. Now, like *The Sot-Weed Factor* itself, it seems alternately grandiloquent and stilted. *Strange*

Peaches addresses itself to more complex material and treats it well, with a humor and a balance that is more difficult to sustain than the archaic style of the earlier book.

What one wonders is whether Mr. Greene, or anyone, has attentively reread those books or any of our literature lately. Or were his choices, like those of the many readers who sigh for *Leaving Cheyenne,* made on the basis of fond memory?

If I suspect the latter, it is because I now know from experience how difficult most Texas books are to reread. There are none that one would want to go back to time and again, and very few that can be read with genuine pleasure even twice.

If *Texas Monthly* wants to do us a real service, it ought to solicit not merely A. C. Greene's list of fifty Texas books, but a listing of the favorite *non-Texas* books of fifty Texas authors. My own sad impression is that there are plenty of Texas authors who haven't read fifty non-Texas books in the last decade. Books about Texas cross my desk constantly and I search them hopefully but in vain for any sign of the author's reading. Where are the borrowings and subtle or not-so-subtle thefts? Where are the echoes, allusions, correspondences, and restatements with which most richly textured books abound? Where, in our books, will one get a sense of a mind actively in contact with other minds, or a style nervously aware of other styles?

Almost nowhere, that's where. The most shocking but also the fairest charge that can be levelled at Texas literature is that it is disgracefully insular and uninformed. Writing is nourished by reading—broad, curious, sustained reading; it flows from a profound alertness, fine-tuned by both literature and life. Perhaps we have not yet sloughed off the frontier notion that reading is idle or sissified. At the moment our books are protein-deficient, though the protein is there to be had, in

other literatures. Until we have better readers it is most unlikely that we will have better writers.

If some of the above seems overstated, it is because I've concluded that nothing short of insult moves people in Texas.
This is perhaps another aspect of clinging frontierism. Gentle
chidings go unheard. In these parts the critical act has never
been accepted, much less honored: literary criticism generally
means two writers having a fistfight in a bar.

Not only do we need critics, we need writers who are
willing to get along without one another's approval. Literary
comradeship is a fine thing up to the point at which it begins to produce a pompous, self-congratulatory, and self-
protective literary culture. In Texas, rampant good-old-
boy-and-girlism has produced exactly that: a pond full of
self-satisfied frogs.

In my opinion the self-satisfaction is entirely unjustified.
There are as yet *no* solid achievements in Texas letters. Those
who fancy otherwise probably haven't tried to reread the
books. Cyril Connolly felt that the minimum one should
ask of a book was that it remain readable for ten years. When
this modest standard is applied to one's Texas books their
ranks are immediately decimated—indeed, almost eliminated,
in view of which it seems the more unfortunate that our in-
state literary culture has begun to exhibit the sort of status-
consciousness characteristic of literary society in New York or
London, without the excuse of talent or anything resembling
the intellectual density to be found in those cities.

The hunter who is reluctant to use a gig might as well
avoid the frog-pond of Texas letters. Gigs are what's needed.
As it is, most Texas writers work for a lifetime without receiving a single paragraph of intent criticism, and if they should
get one now and then it will usually come from out of state.
Anything resembling a tough-minded discussion of Texas

books by a Texan is thought to be unneighborly. The writers get reviewed, but reviews are merely first impressions. Criticism begins as the second impression, or the third, and even the thumbnail variety, which is all I can offer, is almost never practiced here.

The need for hard-nosed, energetic, and unintimidated local critics is plainly urgent. It's one thing that our literary society has gotten so clubby and pompous, quite another that the books which constitute the reason for having a literary society are still predominantly soft, thin, and sentimental—not to mention dull, portentous, stylistically impoverished, and intellectually empty. The large majority of them are dead where they sit, and reading them is about as pleasant as eating sawdust.

In fairness I should point out that I realize this is a condition not unique to Texas. Minnesota hasn't produced a great literature either, nor Idaho, nor perhaps even California. Fortunately I am not from any of those places, and their failings are not my concern.

This brings me to another point, or another aspect of our literary immaturity—i.e., the habit we have of attempting to annex any writer who happens to stray across the state line. Recently I received a prospectus for a bibliography of Texas authors which included such well-known Texas boys as Max Apple (Detroit), Michael Mewshaw (Takoma Park, Maryland), and Willie Morris (Yazoo City, Mississippi).

The inclusion of Willie Morris is particularly amusing, since he has spent much of his life proclaiming—with almost every waking breath—that he is a Mississippian.

Michael Mewshaw has probably spent more time in the south of France than he has in Texas. Does a job at the University of Texas automatically make one a Texas writer? If this strange standard were rigorously applied I would have to consider myself a Virginia writer, since I once held a teaching job there.

There is no point in wasting space on these claims, which are almost never made by the writers themselves. Attempts to bolster our ranks with latecomers or temporary residents won't work. Joyce found it convenient to live much of his life in France. Did this make him a French writer? Beckett even learned to write in French, without, however, ceasing to be Irish.

I am mainly going to hew to the simple rule that only those born and raised in Texas have the dubious honor of literary citizenship. Even writers who become absorbed in the state, and make good use of some part of it—as Beverly Lowry has of Houston, in *Daddy's Girl*—shouldn't have to consider themselves Texas writers. Graham Greene has used a great many places well, while remaining thoroughly English.

The one case that could be called either way is Donald Barthelme, who has lived enough of his life in Texas to be considered a Texas writer if he wants to. Whether such a designation matters to him I have no way of knowing, but what is obvious is that his fiction has no need of Texas. Barthelme is a brilliant, high-risk modernist, who operates on a hairline, with no greater margin of error than that of a lyric poet. In quality, his work has almost no middle. The stories that are perfect are wonderful; those that are off by a millimeter fail completely. He is the one prose writer I know of to whom an analogy to a trapeze artist seems exact: a miss means death. In the best stories, just watching him not miss provides an intellectual excitement so high that it often brings emotion with it. The perfect stories accumulate slowly, usually one or two a year, but Barthelme keeps working; the recently published *Sixty Stories,* despite many misses, is an impressive achievement.

In the hasty survey which follows I am going to concentrate mainly on books published since 1950—it seems to me it has been within this thirty-year span that Texas literature has clearly failed to realize itself. I would prefer to talk mainly about fiction, but see no way to avoid some discussion of the reminiscential literature which has, from the first, been so popular with Texas writers. One explanation for this may be that lying doesn't come easy to children of the frontier. It is ironic that Texans, known the world over for being big liars, still can't lie well enough to write interesting novels, preferring, for the most part, the milder fabrications allowable in reminiscence.

As I said in my previous essay, there is not much Texas fiction earlier than 1950 that needs to be looked at, other than that of Miss Porter. James Phillips's *The Inheritors* (1940) seems wooden as any plank; the same can be said for Edward Anderson's *Thieves Like Us.* George Sessions Perry's fiction is now as dead as the magazines he wrote it for. *Hold Autumn in Your Hand,* his farming novel, seems workaday indeed when compared to Edith Sumners Kelley's *Weeds,* the one masterpiece of this genre.

In general, the best Texas books of this period confuse honesty with artistry. Their writers produced, without self-consciousness, what might be called novels of information, for readers who had not yet grown accustomed to getting their information off a television screen. Such writers told it like it was, but unfortunately didn't tell it very well, and their books now have only a period interest.

In the mid-fifties a considerably more interesting generation began to be heard from, its principal voices being John Graves, William Humphrey, William Goyen, and John Howard Griffin, all of whom differed significantly from the Texas writers who had come before them. In their differing ways they were our first literary aesthetes, the first writers after Miss Porter to feel that literature should be elegant as well as honest. Also, they were internationalists, well educated and well traveled; and all had been to school to the masters of modern literature. They were more likely to echo Faulkner or Joyce or the French Symbolists than to imitate J. Frank Dobie or Roy Bedichek.

The most obvious thing that can be said about this gifted group is that they have not produced very many books. Granting that the three or four best books—*Goodbye to a River, The Ordways, The House of Breath, The Devil Rides Outside*—are among our very best books, it seems nonetheless a slim yield.

Perhaps an admirable desire to put quality over quantity has held their yield down—or then again it may be that in their travels they acquired a rather more Mediterranean outlook on life than is common between the Red River and the Rio Grande. They have managed the nice trick of sustaining their ambitions without being absolutely driven by them, in the process acquiring a balance that may be good for their souls while keeping a brake on their output. John Graves likes to farm, William Humphrey likes to fish, William Goyen enjoys living in L.A., and none seems much interested in slighting their absorbing pursuits in order to write the Great Texas Novel. Each has made it plain that he doesn't intend to be a blind slave to the Protestant work ethic.

Two of them, Griffin and Humphrey, seem to have been pressed into fiction by the force of one compelling traumatic experience, the like of which never happened again. In the case of the late John Howard Griffin, this resulted in an odd, lopsided career, of the sort that often happens when a writer has the always serious, usually fatal misfortune to write his best book first.

The Devil Rides Outside has the lonely distinction of being the best French novel ever published in Fort Worth. It is a strange, strong book whose verbal energy—a quality very rare in our fiction—still seems remarkable after almost thirty years. In the mostly all-too-healthy and sunlit world of Texas fiction, the book remains an anomaly, dark, feverish, introverted, claustrophobic, tortured.

It was so complete and so explosive an outpouring of intellectualized emotion that Griffin seemed, from then on, a sort of emptied man. His second novel, *Nuni*, had neither energy nor force. He then wrote a history of a Midland bank, and finally, perhaps in desperation, turned himself black, in a last effort to find something strong to write about.

There are reports that Griffin left at least one completed novel, perhaps several. When these are published his career may seem less strangely truncated than is the case now.

William Humphrey has had a considerably more satisfying, not to mention more intelligible development. The short stories collected in *The Last Husband,* his first book, were fairly conventional, but did make clear that he was working toward a style of his own, one which was not to mature fully until *The Ordways. Home from the Hill* succeeds to the extent that it does on the strength of the story and is actually somewhat hindered by the style, which had not yet worked itself clear of Southern portentousness and Faulknerian hype.

Full clarity came with *The Ordways,* in 1964, a beautifully crafted novel which turns the traditional family chronicle into a kind of dance of the generations. *The Ordways* is funny, moving, elegantly written and firmly controlled. It was as if a less prolix Thackeray had turned his attention to East Texas, though rather too briefly, as it now appears.

In the succeeding seventeen years Humphrey has produced a couple of fishing books and a graceful memoir, but no more novels. One of the fishing books, *The Spawning Run,* is very charming, but I would still rather have a successor to *The Ordways.* And of course, we may get it. There is no indication that William Humphrey is exhausted, or even tired.

Like Humphrey, William Goyen is an East Texan who adroitly managed to escape both the region and the state. Goyen, too, is a stylist; in fact he is probably more style-obsessed than any Texas writer. It was language, rather than story, that immediately marked *The House of Breath* as something new in Texas letters. There had been no sentences quite that well-considered in our books. Goyen went to school to the French, and worked hard to make his prose as elegant and firm as that of the French masters.

For a few years, at least, he succeeded, and the fact that he succeeded constitutes his most fundamental problem as a novelist. Goyen has the instincts of a prose poet and is slightly resentful of the demands of narrative, with which an extreme concern with style must often be in conflict. His fiction tends to break into moments, or memories, each highly textured and embellished. But in arresting the moment in order to describe it in its fullest intricacy, he also arrests the movement of his story; the prose gathers so much attention to itself that virtually none is left for his characters; in the end one comes away with a sense of having passed through something gorgeous but ultimately vague. This tendency to weave spells with his prose has persisted. Goyen is aware of it and now and then makes an attempt to write more simply, but simplicity is not really his métier. Since his language at its best is beautiful most readers prefer the seductions of the early books to the condescensions of the more recent.

This brings us to John Graves, the nature of whose work seems to me to be a good deal more complicated than it is popularly thought to be. Thanks partly to his geniality, partly to his relative accessibility, and partly to the fact that he writes about the country, Graves has to some degree been made heir to the Dobie-Webb-Bedichek tradition, with the surely unwelcome responsibility of keeping that branch of Texas letters vital.

That he is quite restive in this role is constantly apparent in his writing; one of his most frequent rhetorical devices, used almost to the point of abuse, is to undercut himself: questioning a story he has just retold, doubting an observation he has just made, twisting out from under a position. Often he simply reverses his field and abandons whatever line of thought he has been pursuing.

He is popularly thought to be a kind of country explainer, when in fact he seems more interested in increasing

our store of mysteries than our store of knowledge. He loves
the obscure, indeterminate nature of rural legend and likes
nothing better than to retell stories the full truth of which
can never be known. If nature continues to stimulate him it
may be because it too is elusive, feminine, never completely
knowable.

Certainly he is not looking forward to becoming the Sage
of Glen Rose. His best writing is based on doubt and ambiva-
lence—or at least two-sidedness; he is not eager to arrive at
too many certainties, or any certainty too quickly. The persona he adopts most frequently is that of the man who *considers.* He may choose to consider a goat, a book, an anecdote, or
some vagary of nature, but the process of considering is more
important to the texture of his books than any conclusions that
may get drawn.

John Graves differs from many Texas writers in that,
apart from a few short stories, he did not publish his appren-
tice work; instead he sprang into view full-grown in *Goodbye
to a River,* a book that represents not so much an abandonment
of fiction as a form of accommodation with it. Though based
on a real trip, it is essentially an imaginary voyage whose
affinities stretch back to *Gulliver* and beyond. What strikes one
about it today is not the natural description, but the harshness
of the experience which the traveler recapitulates. It is rich in
massacres and feuds, old angers and bitter defeats.

The gentle style in which these angers and defeats are
described is an end product whose beginnings are hidden in
the unpublished fiction. It is a lovely style whose one disadvantage is that it tends to suck the rawness out of experiences which need to remain raw if they are to be fully felt. An
idiom that is perfect for a boat trip won't necessarily serve for
a massacre. The cogency of *Goodbye to a River,* and the fact that
it encompasses in concentrated form so much that is central to
Graves's experience and feeling, has left him with the problem
of extension: how to go beyond himself? This is a problem all

writers eventually come to, but the writer who starts late and starts well is apt to feel it more acutely.

Looking at it hard, these four talents—Humphrey and Goyen, Graves and Griffin—produced between them only six or seven keepable books in some twenty-five years, which is not exactly spinning them out. Add to that the list of Texas writers who have so far produced only *one* book and a view emerges of a literary climate productive either of early blight or extreme constipation.

The one-bookers would include William Brammer, William Casey, Hughes Rudd, Tom Horn, Dorothy Yates, Walter Clemons, Mack Williams, Sherry Kafka, and probably numbers of others whose one book I can't find. Of these Brammer and Casey are dead, Rudd and Clemons busy at other tasks; the rest, so far as one can tell, simply stopped. None of their first books was an absolute heartstopper, yet each had some strength and some appeal, good enough to encourage one to look for the next book. *My Escape from the C.I.A.* and *The Poison Tree* each contain one or two excellent short stories; *A Shroud for a Journey, The Shallow Grass,* and *Hannah Jackson* are the sort of first novels that seem to promise development. All that one can say is that it hasn't happened.

The only book by the one-bookers that still enjoys any currency is *The Gay Place.* Bill Brammer is not the first writer to lose control of his life before gaining full control of his art, but his loss is one Texas readers might justly lament the most. He brought to our letters an easy and natural urbanity then almost unknown in these parts. Also, he was fortunate in his moment: the flea circus of state politics as it existed in Johnsonian Austin was the perfect feeding ground for his talent. He was alert, curious, and witty, happy to use the absurdities which lay so abundantly to hand; and, in the end, just romantic enough to make it all seem more charming and less destructive than it really was. But *The Gay Place* is material searching for design. Brammer had the talents and disposition of a Silver Poet—our Catullus, not our Balzac—and the big novel demanded by the age was the wrong form for him. He could neither resist nor control his material and so buried an elegant small novel about capitol debaucheries and the pathos of ambition in a large confused book about a little bit of everything. Still, of all our beginnings that turned out to be endings, it remains the most appealing.

A word, now, about the journalists. A great many Texas writers have come out of journalism, in particular sportswriting. Brammer came out of it, for example, and fairly far out. The classic analysis of the dangers of journalism to a writer who aspires to move beyond it was made by Leonard Woolf, in *Beginning Again*, pages 132–35. It is too long to quote: suffice to say that it is very brilliant and very accurate. The journalist trains to write something which will be read once and thrown away. Moreover, the writing will generally have to compete with eggs and bacon and the chatter of the domestic breakfast table. To do such writing successfully requires no mean skill— but it does need skills different from those required if one is competing with Shakespeare and Tolstoy, or Hemingway and Faulkner, or—to come on home—William Humphrey and John Graves.

    In reading through the books of our several journalist-novelists, I have come to think that a crucial problem has to do with an attitude toward readers. The journalists are usually smart and quite often write excellent prose, but all are insecure in relation to readers. Trained to write columns that can be read in a few seconds, or articles that take at most a few minutes, in their novels they seem desperate to *affect* the reader every few seconds, or at least every minute or two.

    But, obviously, novels aren't columns, their rhythms are often extremely long ones, and the reader's attention—if it is to be held—must be allowed varying levels of intensity. A rata-tat-tat effect, with a joke, an *aperçu,* or a dazzling rhetorical move every few lines, quickly becomes intolerable in a novel.

This tendency is particularly noticeable in the work of Edwin Shrake, in my view the best of our journalist-novelists. Shrake has always been an intriguing talent, far superior to most of his drinking buddies. He has energy, skill, imagination, and persistence. Not many writers start out with a paperback Western (*Blood Reckoning*) and go on to update *The Satyricon,* as he does in *Peter Arbiter.* All of his books begin well, and yet all are difficult to finish, in my view because Shrake can't resist the constant hit. He is a genuinely funny writer with no sense of how to space effects—being funny too often in the same vein is as bad as not being funny at all. Perhaps I'm wrong, but this seems to be a holdover from sportswriting, since much the same thing happens in the (to me) much less interesting fiction of Dan Jenkins and Gary Cartwright. In a novel, trying to keep the reader alert every single second is the one sure way to insure that the reader will go to sleep.

Larry King's prose suffers a little from this same tendency, but since the basic unit of his work is the magazine article he frequently gets away with it. He has a strong, vivid style that works well when one considers his pieces in isolation, in the magazines where most of them appeared. When these pieces are then gathered into collections it is evident that he tends to splash the same colors and repeat certain characteristic verbal devices a good deal too often.

He has written an acute piece about playing cowboy, without perhaps noting that he constantly does just that in his prose—though he *has* written ruefully and perceptively of the effects of writing everything to a deadline. As his career advanced, he began to make himself a character in his own reportage, sometimes too self-consciously, in the manner of Mailer. Perhaps naturally, he is more of a presence in these pieces than many of the people he was sent to report on. Read

from start to finish, his collected journalism is a kind of reverse *Pilgrim's Progress,* with Larry being the rather aggressive
pilgrim, at large in contemporary life.

Unfortunately, very little of this work has made any demands on his emotions. Consequently, when his emotions are
tapped, as in the brief, beautiful essay on his father called
"The Old Man," the effect is wonderful and makes us wish it
weren't so uncommon. "The Old Man" puts everything else
he has written in the deep shade. Now that *The Best Little
Whorehouse* has freed him from journalism one hopes more of
that kind of work will result.

Something ought to be said, I suppose, not merely about *The
Best Little Whorehouse* but also about the second most popular
Texas drama, Preston Jones's *Texas Trilogy.* What I can say is
that I found the latter obnoxious on almost every level, but
principally on the level of dialogue and attitude. The dialogue,
with its numerous adjectival "By-gods," is collegiate-suburban
Country-Western, as affected as Tom McGuane's ghastly dialogue in *The Missouri Breaks.* The three plays are simply little
strings of weakly dramatized anecdotage, appealing mainly to
those who like to think sweet thoughts about Texas small
towns. Both the musical and the *Trilogy* succeed to the extent
that they do by sentimentalizing small-town life, though the
article from which Larry King derived the musical is by no
means sentimental.

There are, so far as I know, only four Texas writers who have
been able to reverse the tendency toward nostalgia, sentiment,
and small-town mythicization. These are Terry Southern, Max
Crawford, James Crumley, and John Irsfeld.

The first, Terry Southern, escaped quickly and devoted
only a few stories to Texas, but these few have an edge that at
the time was rare. *The Magic Christian* and *Red Dirt Marijuana*
are good enough to make one regret that Southern seems to

have left fiction for screenwriting. Slowing down just when they should be speeding up is too common a pattern with our writers.

Crumley, Crawford, and Irsfeld are to our fiction what Willie and Waylon were to our music before they got popular. In a state that overrates almost every writer who publishes a book, they have managed the rare feat of being not only underrated, but almost unknown. *One to Count Cadence* and *The Last Good Kiss* (Crumley), *The Backslider* and *Waltz across Texas* (Crawford), and *Little Kingdoms* and *Coming Through* (Irsfeld) are our Outlaw books, critical, hardbitten, disrespectful to the point of contempt. Instead of having a love-hate relationship with the old state, these writers mostly just hate it. When they look at the small town, they look at it as critically as Samuel Butler looked at the Victorian family. In contemplating Texas life they are unawed, almost to the point of savagery, and the fact that they enjoy complete neglect is not making them any tamer. The folksy satire of the *Texas Trilogy* or *The Best Little Whorehouse* is like sugar candy in comparison to the Swiftian acids of *Waltz across Texas* or *The Backslider*.

All three men are smart, tough, skilled, and educated; also, they are geared to fiction as naturally as the writers of an earlier generation were geared to journalism or reminiscence, or both. Unfortunately a literary climate poisonous to fiction and favorable to journalism has already to some extent retarded their development, and may stop it altogether, unless they're lucky. I hope they survive—our fiction needs the critical element as badly as the trans-Pecos needs rain.

And what of that odd trio of writers who are alike in nothing except that they inhabit the trans-Pecos: Tom Lea, John Rechy, and Elroy Bode?

If Tom Lea reaches the next generation of Texans it will likely be as an artist. He has a good eye but a poor ear; the more his characters talk the less convincing his fiction becomes. He is more interesting visually than verbally. Both *The Wonderful Country* and *The Hands of Cantú* contain excellent descriptive writing but fail to create characters of much depth or much interest.

Ear, on the other hand, was John Rechy's major strength. *City of Night* remains a readable first book precisely because he rendered what he had heard and seen so perfectly, with such fine attention to costume, expression, and idiom. But he wrote it in practically the last moment before the description of sexual lifestyles became clichéd and then passé. Though certainly aware of this development, Rechy has not been inventive enough to sidestep it, and has basically repeated himself, with ever-diminishing returns.

Elroy Bode is our minimalist, a confirmed nostalgic who has pinned his hopes on prose style. Fortunately for him, his is attractive, at least in the short sketches in which he exposes it. Like planes that fly under radar, the sketch slides under criticism. You either like them or you don't. Quite a few of Bode's are very appealing, though an equal number seem mannered and precious. Come upon individually, in magazines, the sketches often delight; reading them in the aggregate, in books, is not so pleasing. One gets tired of his taking every little Texas thing he bumps into quite so seriously. A really good book will seem to be more than the sum of its parts, but a collection of sketches only adds up to the sum of the very best sketches, which may constitute only twenty percent of the book. One admires Bode's individualism, while wishing he weren't so locked into a form whose resources he has long since exhausted.

It is hard to say much about the reminiscers, of whom there have been a great many. It all depends upon the quality of the mind that's doing the reminiscing, and down here the quality has been, if not pedestrian, at least quite conventional. An intellectual autobiography on the order of *The Education of Henry*

Adams would be nice to have, but we don't have one. Our reminiscers tend to be nostalgic and simplistic, interested mainly in paying tribute to colorful ancestors and vanished lifestyles. A few charm, most bore. They are valuable insofar as they provide grist for the historian, pernicious to the extent that they encourage reaction and ruralism.

Texas consists of dozens of subregions, many of which have prompted a novel or two. I am partial, for example, to Jack Sheridan's *Thunderclap* (1952), largely because it happens to be set in the much-neglected Wichita Falls–Vernon area. Natives of other subregions can doubtless name similar books, most of which do little more than provide field notes to the subregion. I once had the misfortune to see a list of some 350 books about Texas—novels, mostly—compiled by an earnest but misguided researcher. It consisted of 345 dead books and four or five whose vital signs were growing ever more faint.

For that matter, six of my own eight books seem to have stopped breathing in the last few years. I am not surprised. It took me until around 1972 to write a book that an intelligent reader might want to read twice, and by 1976 I had once again lost the knack. There is nothing very remarkable in this: writing novels is not a progressive endeavor. One might get better, one might get worse. If I'm lucky and industrious I might recover the knack, or then again I might be very industrious and never recover it. There is always that gamble involved in writing. Too many writers, in Texas and out, have been coddled into believing that art is a more acceptable, less obdurate thing than it actually is. It is quite difficult to write a book that an intelligent reader will want to read twice, and near and not-so-near misses are the rule, rather than the exception.

Some misses trouble one more than others. The flubbed Texas book that bothers me the most is Robert Flynn's *North to Yesterday*. Flynn had a world-class idea—Cervantes's idea; a *Don Quixote* of the trail drives—but it was his first book and his powers weren't adequate to the visionary tragicomedy that would have done justice to it. He had the right material, but at the wrong time.

There are at least a couple of dozen Texas writers I haven't considered in this essay. There is the late Ben K. Green, hopefully the last and certainly the most pretentious of the yarners. Then there are Robert Flynn and Al Dewlen, Benjamin Capps and C. W. Smith, Shelby Hearon, Warren Leslie, Marshall Terry, Dillon Anderson, Nolan Porterfield, Allen Wier, Leonard Sanders, Suzanne Morris, Madison Cooper, Peter Gent, and a host of others. Fatigue, rather than charity, inclines me to pass them without extensive comment, though I will say that *Sironia, Texas* is the book that makes the best doorstop. Some of the rest have talent, but none so far has used it to write a book likely to last ten years. Most get by, to the extent that they do, on modest capacities for straight-grain narrative realism. They are storytellers who tell ordinary stories rather ordinarily. If this seems harsh, pick up any one of their books and try reading it. There will be numerous passages that charm, but no book that compels acute attention. A. C. Greene's attempt to make a case for *I and Claudie* is so much mouthwash.

The other day it occurred to me, apropos of nothing, that the millennium is only eighteen years away. Horses routinely live eighteen years, but books don't. It is quite possible that no book written in Texas in the last two or three decades will still seem worth reading eighteen years hence.

The problem is not so much shallow talent as shallow commitment. Our best writers' approach to art is tentative and intermittent: half-assed, to put it bluntly. Instead of an infinite capacity for taking pains they develop an infinite capacity for avoiding work, and employ their creativity mainly to convince themselves that they are working well when in fact they are hardly working at all. The majority of our most talented writers have not yet produced even one book with a real chance of lasting. Forget second acts in Texas literature: so far we have only a bare handful of credible *first* acts.

Meanwhile, as the cities boom and the state changes, a great period is being wasted. Fiction in particular thrives on transitions, on the destruction of one lifestyle by another. Houston and Dallas have sucked in thousands of Rubempres, but where are the books about them? These cities are dripping experience, but instead of sopping up the drippings and converting them into literature our writers mainly seem to be devoting themselves to an ever more self-conscious countrification.

There is no point in belaboring the obvious. Until Texas writers are willing to work harder, inform themselves more broadly, and stop looking only backward, we won't have a literature of any interest.

That said, I want to reverse my thrust and pay tribute in closing to the one Texas writer for whose work I have an unequivocal admiration: that is, Vassar Miller. *Adam's Footprint* was published in 1956, and from that time until rather recently Miller has been the one poet of genuine distinction in the state. I think it no hyperbole to suggest that her dozen best poems will outlast all the books mentioned in this essay, plus the fifty on A. C. Greene's list as well. That she is to this day little-known, read, or praised in Texas is the most damning comment possible on our literary culture. She works in the hardest form—the lyric poem, the form where the percentage of failure is inevitably highest. Many of hers do fail, of course, but the ones which succeed come as close as any writing done in Texas to achieving what can fairly be called excellence: the product of a high gift wedded to long-sustained and exceedingly rigorous application.

I am not seeking to sanctify her, but merely to point out that we do have one very gifted writer who has continued for some thirty years to do what a writer is supposed to do: write.

Adam's Footprint and the volumes which succeed it are among the very few Texas books to which one can, with confidence, always return. There is definitely a there there: hard-won, high, intelligent, felt, finished, profound. To Vassar Miller, if to anyone we have, belongs the laurel.

Postscript, 1987

The main thing I regret about this essay is the title. The phrase I had in mind, of course, was "ever a bridesmaid." Well, the fingers that do the typing don't always cooperate perfectly with the brain that does the thinking—*if* it's thinking.

Recently, in another context, I typed "marriage" when I meant to type "marijuana." The slips are probably Freudian, but even if they're not Freudian, they're ominous.

I've been mildly surprised that, in this age of feminism, no one has written to ask whether I really meant "ever a bridesmaid," and if not, why not.

Once into the essay itself, things seem to go more smoothly. I have a few regrets. One is the omission of Elmer Kelton. I should have read him then, but I didn't. I'm just now reading him. If it's any consolation to Elmer, I'm just getting around to Goethe, too.

I also regret questioning Donald Barthelme's credentials as a Texan. I now know them to be impeccable. And if anyone got skimped in my assessment, it was Barthelme, whose achievement looms larger and ever larger and whose work contains the kinds of refreshments and surprises which draw one back to it. And when one goes back, one finds more than one had noticed the first time.

The exact opposite must be said for most Texas writers. It's dangerous to revisit their books—one usually finds less than one had supposed was there.

As for the general critique, it seems gentle to me now.

(Actually, it seemed gentle to me then.) There finally just isn't very much that repays a second look. The older talents may not be slowing down, but neither are they speeding up. They go along, much as they were, and the younger talents seem rather flat. If a Texas book has appeared which just seems to be bursting with youth, originality, and energy, I've missed it.

The one area where there's been a clear advance is—as this volume makes clear—in criticism. There *is* criticism now—a very welcome and very belated development.

When I wrote the essay I meant to be provocative, and I hoped to be tough-minded. The provocation yielded a thin harvest—some routine bad-mouthings and moderate-to-sour grapes. And the tough-mindedness just really isn't there. I pulled too many punches; the final effect is mild.

HORSEMAN, HANG ON: THE REALITY OF MYTH IN TEXAS LETTERS

Craig Clifford

> Anticipation of one's uttermost and ownmost possibility is coming back understandingly to one's ownmost "been."
>
> —Martin Heidegger, *Being and Time*

As a displaced Texan living in Maryland and an unemployed Ph.D. in philosophy, I was lucky enough to meet a displaced Irishman who dared to challenge my Lone Star credentials. After five years in Buffalo, New York, and a couple in Annapolis, Maryland, I had become downright obnoxious about being a Texan—having, for example, repeatedly threatened the lives of unsuspecting Yankees who suggested that a Texas accent sounds stupid, or that all Southern accents are the same, or that Northeastern universities are superior to Southern ones—so I thought myself well beyond reproach on that score.

At a picnic given by the English department in which my wife was teaching, I had almost given up on hearing about anything other than the mechanics of publishing articles and securing research grants when I noticed someone who didn't seem to fit. He noticed my wife and me about the same time, so a conversation was inevitable. He was stocky and tan, sort of an outdoors Norman Mailer at forty, and when we asked

---

This essay was first published in the 10 February 1982 issue of the *Texas Observer* and was later included in Craig Clifford's *In the Deep Heart's Core: Reflections on Life, Letters, and Texas* (Texas A&M University Press, 1985).

what he did, he said that he kept the grounds. He asked about us, and he seemed particularly interested to hear that my wife taught poetry. He wanted to know which poets. My wife, figuring that a groundskeeper probably wouldn't have heard of any poets she might name, said that she taught the epic tradition.

"Do you do any Yeets?" he asked.

"You mean Yeats?"

"Yeah."

Next thing you know he was asking her about half a dozen books on Yeats and expounding on the remarkable growth that is evident in Yeats's work right up to his death.

"Sounds like you've spent some time with Yeats."

"I guess about fifteen years." He took another swig of his beer, rocked back on his heels, and came out with the following barrage in the purest Irish brogue:

> Under bare Ben Bulben's head
> In Drumcliff churchyard Yeats is laid.
> An ancestor was rector there
> Long years ago, a church stands near,
> By the road an ancient cross.
> No marble, no conventional phrase;
> On limestone quarried near the spot
> By his command these words are cut:
>
> *Cast a cold eye*
> *On life, on death.*
> *Horseman, pass by!*

My wife and I looked at each other as if to say, I guess "Yeets" was a joke. Our poetry-steeped gardener, it seemed, had come over from Ireland in his early teens with his father, himself a renowned Irish short-story writer.

There was, however, a second surprise. Somewhere in the midst of drinking ourselves into the woodwork and exalting the virtues of Yeats, my wife and I mentioned that we were from Texas. When our drunken poetic gardener heard that, he immediately listed off the top of his head at least a dozen books on Texas or by Texans that I had never heard of—"How can you call yourself a Texan if you haven't read . . . ?" I insisted that I *was* one, so I didn't need to read about them; but that was as untrue to my philosophical experience as it was to the soil that had nurtured me for the first twenty years of my life.

Emotionally I had already recognized the power of that soil. Although most expatriates don't get the severe kind of homesickness until they reach forty or fifty, at the ripe young age of twenty-nine I was already to the point where the sound of Bill Moyers's accent was enough to drive me to drink.

But these inarticulate yearnings needed articulation. In a sense, I was already looking for a way back to Texas. I had spent ten years studying Martin Heidegger, a twentieth-century philosopher whose thought is so thoroughly rooted in the dark hills of the Black Forest of southern Germany that those who study him are forced either to ape his way of speaking or to return to their own *Heimat* for strength and inspiration. I had spent years reading Heidegger's reflections on the significance of place, on "dwelling poetically," on the way in which man "is as having been," on the way in which understanding what I have been is the only way to understand what I can and cannot be; but I had never fully applied these reflections to myself. The fact of the matter is, I didn't have a way to do that, not until a poetry-crazed Irishman—who, it turned out, had spent ten years in New Mexico studying the role of the Irish in the Southwest—force-fed me Walter Prescott Webb, John Graves, and Larry McMurtry.

But then again, perhaps I'm getting carried away. Is it anything more than pure romanticism to think that someone who grew up on the outskirts of Houston in the second half of the twentieth century, someone who has spent more time studying Greek philosophy and German poetry than punching cattle, could learn who he is by reading how Captain L. H. McNelly crossed the Rio Grande with thirty Texas Rangers in 1875 against all orders of the U.S. authorities? Isn't it a mite farfetched to think that any of the rapidly increasing numbers of urban Texans could learn something about themselves by reading McMurtry's tales of the dying breaths of the old-time Texas ranchers?

After all, McMurtry himself abandoned the rural themes of his earlier novels long ago, and, having sufficiently elegized the passing of the frontier in his 1968 book of essays, he has counseled Texas writers to turn to the cities, most forcefully in his 1981 *Texas Observer* piece condemning the continuing infatuation of Texans with the cowboy myth. Texans now are city people—the death of the cowboy has been sufficiently lamented, and the new fodder for Texas literature should come from Dallas and Houston, not Archer County. In fact, McMurtry assures us, the ol' home on the range was not all that it's been cracked up to be anyway. He has repeatedly criticized the Big Three of Texas letters—Dobie, Webb, and Bedichek—for their tendency to romanticize the frontier life. His accounts, he leads us to believe, stay closer to the realities of Texas life, even when that reality is not so pleasant, even when, God forbid, he should find himself forced to criticize Texas.

To romanticize, then, means to falsify—that is, to let the myths get the upper hand on the reality. A. C. Greene echoes this sentiment: "The myth won't let Texas inspect itself with reality. It is impossible to write a novel about Texas using only so-called ordinary people. A 'Texas' character must be included." And Wallace Stegner, though a superb craftsman in the realm of Western myth, nonetheless elevates reality over myth when he addresses this issue explicitly: "The real people of the West are infrequently cowboys and never myths. . . . They confront the real problems of real life in a real region." Myth here means falsehood.

And yet, whether it was romanticism or not, whether or not I entered the realm of myth, when I read how McNelly told a U.S. Cavalry officer that he didn't object to his men sitting down with him because he wouldn't fight alongside anyone he didn't believe his equal, I knew a little better than I did before why I'm the way I am. The fact of the matter is, I do identify myself as a Texan, even if I don't know how to explain what that is. The fact of the matter is, after reading about Captain McNelly, I was in a lot better position to say what a Texan is than I was before. Even if I was an urbanite, I knew a lot better why a Texas urbanite is different from a New York one. And not just in reading about McNelly—but also in reading about the Texas Rangers who got out of hand in Reynosa in 1846, or about the Texans who insisted on driving all of the Reserve Indians out of the state in 1859, or even about Hud Bannon.

The plain fact of the matter is, being a Texan is itself a mythic reality. It is not merely that I grew up within the bounds of the appropriate three rivers, but rather, having grown up there, I *am* a certain way. In order to say what it is that appeals to me about some of the contemporary Texas writers, and, for that matter, about the old ones too, I have to take issue with the bifurcation of myth and reality with which McMurtry, Greene, Stegner, and company defend themselves—for two reasons, one philosophical and one geographical. I wouldn't propose to quibble with McMurtry's pronouncements on the merits and shortcomings of this or that Texas author. Concerning the books I know, I agree with quite a bit of what he has to say—so long as I keep a steady supply of grains of salt on hand. Instead, I propose to disagree about some of the fundamentals.

If the entity we call "Texas" involves the interaction of places and peoples, it is not so easy to discard all myth as falsehood: when it comes to man, throwing out the myth has something of the character of throwing the pots out with the dishwater. Human reality includes the way in which people understand themselves and their history, and that understanding, to a large extent, involves myth. Yes, I *am* a certain way because I grew up with the idea that Texans are supposed to be a certain way, but there is no such thing as the pure person stripped of the various ideas of what he should be.

The Greek *mythos* means, quite simply, "story." The history of a people includes the tradition of *mythoi* in which that people passes down its history. Reality includes myth, even the myths which patently falsify historical events. Even if Billy the Kid was a ruthless, cold-blooded murderer, the legend of Billy the Kid is nonetheless part of the West, along with the countless *mythoi* which immortalize Western heroes of old who well deserve the honor.

The character of a people is always inextricably bound up with the stories of that people. In the end, Texas itself is a mythic entity, and it wouldn't be anything if it wasn't. Whether there are observable characteristics of Texans which distinguish them from Cajuns and Okies and New Mexicans is largely irrelevant: without the continuing reality of its history, Texas would be nothing—and that history is full of myths and itself survives through the making and remaking of myth, through the telling of that history.

That's just it—the remaking of myth. The implication is not that we should go on believing that Billy the Kid is someone worthy of emulation. We should damn well know that he wasn't, although we should also try to understand what it means that time and again we mythologize such figures in the way we do. The need for the outlaw hero, even if that hero is often used for despicable purposes, bespeaks a deep-seated cultural reality.

So how does one go about remaking a myth? If I may turn to something one of my teachers once said about an eminent storyteller of ancient times, perhaps I can make the point clear. The standard interpretation of the use of myth by Plato has it that Plato carried the world out of the realm of primitive *mythos* into the realm of civilized *logos,* with *mythos* understood as myth in the modern sense and *logos* as reason. As it were, this is the myth of Plato's treatment of myth. My teacher suggested, and after many years of work I found the suggestion well borne out, that the more truthful account would be that Plato moved from one level of myth through reason to a higher level of myth—from *mythos* through *logos* back to *mythos.* Plato's dialogues themselves are mythic in character, not discursive, but they are myths which grew out of a deeply insightful and reflective mind. Plato worked with a tradition of poetic myth and attempted to deepen the myths, *to make the myths more truthful.* One myth among others is the modern myth of the bare fact: that myth is a bad one. The key is to get the myth right, not to do away with it. The key is to tell the story as well as you can, not to throw out the story and hope that reality will be left over.

Some of the contemporary Texas writers are attempting to put forward better myths than the Big Three did, and they might well have done it. Some contemporary writers are attempting to tell the story of Texas better than Hollywood did, and, with some notable Hollywood exceptions, they may well have done it. But they too are telling the story. Even the historian who attempts to recount history as it really happened has to tell the story, for you don't get the history without the story. Once again, the root meaning is suggestive. *Historia,* the Greek word from which we get both "history" and "story," means "inquiry": history in the sense of telling the story of the past is really an inquiry. Even when we try to describe the purely physical characteristics of a geographical region—for example, Stegner's point about the shortage of water in the West—we can't just give the facts, the so-called reality, as they are or it is. The reality as it is can be given in a book, in a poem, in a song, but only to the extent that it has been spoken of, written about, or sung—and in that case, the speaker, writer, or singer has chosen to tell the story, describe the region, in a particular way. There is no such thing as telling the story or describing the region in no particular way.

Stegner, to stick to my example, would like to balance the idea of open possibility which has been the meaning of the West for several hundred years with the idea of *limitation* or *deprivation,* and he's right. What he does, however, is deepen the mythic dimension in which the West is understood, by itself and by the rest of the world. It is a fact of nature, to be sure, that there is less rain west of the 100th meridian. Stegner is making the experience of this deprivation part of the mythic reality that exists at the intersection of Western geography and human understanding, contriving, and caretaking.* Part of the experience of the West is the paradox of plenitude and deprivation. One basis of the bad myth is that Easterners looked upon the West as the land of endless opportunity because they intended only to rape the land for all it was worth, not to live on it. But Westerners themselves, that is, people who went west, also propagated this bad myth. Stegner is trying to offer a better one. In this sense, the West takes on a greater symbolic character for humankind in general, in that it is part of the reality of the West to appear boundless in its resources, even though it is severely limited in one essential resource, water, and just as limited as anywhere else in many others. We have learned, or we should have learned, that the open spaces of the West only gave us a false impression that we could plunder and pollute without noticeable consequence. The vast expanses of the Texas plains, the awesome spectacle of the Rockies, could offer us an experience of the smallness of

---

*It is worth noting here that Stegner is writing in the tradition of Webb's *The Great Plains* (1931) and John Wesley Powell's *Report on the Lands of the Arid Region of the United States* (1878). If you don't have the patience for *The Great Plains,* look at Webb's "The American West: Perpetual Mirage," *Harper's,* May 1957.

the trials and tribulations of mechanized man, rather than the illusion of limitless opportunity for human manipulation and consumption—nature as a symbol of the inexhaustible meaning of being, rather than the inexhaustible availability of raw materials for so-called human purposes. If we learn this, and tell it, the myths which make up part of the reality of the West will deepen. And, with regard to this particular issue, the story of the West is the story of America—as it were, of Western civilization as a whole.

I said I had two reasons to take issue with the bifurcation of myth and reality. To sum up the philosophical one: any entity which includes the involvement of man includes a mythic aspect in its reality. That is as true of New York City or Omaha or England or Germany as it is of Texas. But I've also verged on my second reason, which I originally labeled geographical. After my Irish friend had put me through a crash course in Texas writers, I spent a few weeks in Texas dancing the two-step and doing all those things that Texans are supposed to do. When I got back to Maryland, I wrote a piece about dancing the two-step in Texas and trying to dance the two-step in Maryland and hurriedly sent copies to several of my friends living in various parts of the world. I expected a friend who grew up on a farm in Oklahoma and teaches philosophy at a university in the Midwest to fare better with the cowboy lore than some of my friends from more foreign parts. It turned out that he identified with the tension between the power of place and the denial of place which the life of the intellect tends to create, but not so much with the cowboy lore. In fact, even though the tension he experiences stems in part from the conflict between the superficial complexities of the academic shuffle and the simplicity of dirt farming in Oklahoma, it is less a matter of place for him. "There is something so magical, so mythical, about uttering 'Texas,'" he wrote to me. "'Oklahoma' doesn't have this mythical richness."

Every place has a mythical character. The "spirit of place," to borrow Lawrence Durrell's favorite expression, is alive and well beyond the boundaries of Texas, to be sure. Since leaving Texas, I've lived in Buffalo, New York, in Heidelberg, West Germany, and in Annapolis, Maryland: if all of the prejudice I experienced against a Texas drawl in Buffalo (along with all of my prejudice against Yankee ways in general) and all of the predilection for deck shoes and revulsion against cowboy boots in Annapolis (along with my total inability to act as if I'm from an aristocratic family that was living in Annapolis when Thomas Jefferson used to sail his catamaran on the Chesapeake Bay) and that funny way of talking they have over there in Germany aren't evidence enough, then I don't know what would be. Every place has its myth and its magic, but Texas, if you will, has a little more than its share. Everybody else acknowledges that it does, so why don't we just grin and bear it? That accounts both for its greatness and for its greatest screw-ups. And Texas is more mythical in character because of its rich history. I don't want to produce an elaborate encomium on Texas history—the point is, spirits inhabit any place, and there are a hell of a lot of them in Texas, good and bad, like it or not. If you want to know what it means to be a Texan, and why Texans are the way they are, then you have to find out about all of those spirits who rise up out of those blood- and beer-soaked plains, whether our writers give them voice or not: all of the ones we learned about in school, Houston, Travis, and company; along with the ones we didn't hear too much about in school, like Captain McNelly, Big Foot Wallace, and Chief Bowles of the Cherokees; and even the ones we didn't hear anything about in school, like Martha Sherman and Juan Seguin. It's because of all of that and all of them that the word "Texas" means what it does, and that it is possible for it to mean something it shouldn't.

In other words, to answer McMurtry's charge, whether contemporary Texas writers choose urban or rural settings, they must take account of the overpowering presence of the rural tradition in Texas culture. It is precisely this tradition, it is the inexhaustibility of the cowboy myth, which distinguishes Texas from other places and gives it the special character that it has. Does McMurtry really want Texas writers to go whole-hog cosmopolitan? I've spent over a decade among the cosmopolitans—I've even wandered the streets of McMurtry's beloved Georgetown—and it strikes me that McMurtry himself has fled the specter of cowboy idolatry only to run amuck in another form of romanticization—cosmopolitanism. If McMurtry has encountered more than his share of cowboy romanticizers, I've had more experience with Texas intellectuals and pseudointellectuals who would rather be mugged and raped on the streets of New York than be caught dead reading a book about rural Texas. Certainly Texas writers need to go to school to the world masters (forgive me if I don't kowtow to the French), and not just to the Big Three of Texas letters; but they do need to go to school to the frontier tradition of Texas one way or another, for that past, not unlike the past of Faulkner's Mississippi, is neither dead nor past. No one today can simply become a cowboy of the nineteenth century, but it's the past which forms the web of possibility out of which we fashion our futures, whether knowingly or not. Texas writers should help us become the best which our tradition offers, not just tell us what we happen to be now. In all fairness I should point out here that Stegner, in spite of his adherence to a strict dichotomy between myth and reality in the passage I quoted earlier, does not share McMurtry's myopic vision of the novelist's relation to history. He challenges the Western writer, not to choose between past and present, but to connect them:

> In the old days, in blizzardy weather, we used to tie a string of lariats from house to barn so as to make it from shelter to responsibility and back again. With personal,

family, and cultural chores to do, I think we had better rig up such a line between past and present. If we do, the term "western literature" will be enlarged beyond its ordinary limitations, and its accomplishments not so easily overlooked.

As I see it, Texas can never really be urban, for our urban centers are infused with rural myths, with the very anti-urbanism which McMurtry wishes to purge from Texas letters: Houston has become a hell of a mess, but it will never be urban the way a Northeastern city is. In fact, it is my impression, after a good spell among the great cities of the Northeast and a few too many experiences with the attempts of Texas cities to become fully urban, that it is twentieth-century urban life which has exhausted itself, and that American writers are rightfully attempting to reestablish a sense of the soil and the land, albeit a new one infused with the experience of urbanization and all of the lessons we've learned about the romanticization of urban life.

Great writers are never really writing about present fact: ironically, precisely because they deal in human possibility, their province—and, as Willie Morris puts it, their burden—is memory. The Great Texas Novel—accepting for the purposes of argument that it hasn't been written—will take on the mythic tradition of Texas in a way that shows us the profound dimension of the human spirit which that tradition continues to represent for Texans and non-Texans alike. The way for Texans to address the universal themes of the human spirit is indeed to learn from the masters, to take their own art seriously, to eschew good-old-boyism and back-patting among the Lone Star philistines, *and*—now that all that's said and done—to face their own tradition squarely and thoughtfully.

I can't help but think of the hours and hours I spent discussing *High Noon* with a professor of Slavic languages at the University of Heidelberg, in Germany. And I can't help but think of the old lady living at the bottom of the hill in Todt-

nauberg where Martin Heidegger had written his greatest
works. She had never heard of Pennsylvania or Baltimore,
where my companions were from, but she lit up like a Christ-
mas tree when she heard the word "Texas." "Cowboys und
Indians, nicht?" As I walked up toward Heidegger's hut, I was
thinking about how rooted in those hills Heidegger's thought
was and how unrooted in my plains mine was. The point is,
the Texas myth continues to pull at a powerful strand in the
human psyche and not just at the pocketbooks of faddish, nostalgic Texas urbanites. Dime novels in Europe and bad Hollywood movies, mechanical bulls and quick-selling paperback
Westerns—these are perversions, to be sure, but they are perversions *of* something, and it is that something that we should
be after. The question is not whether the subject has been exhausted, but whether it has been dealt with with the kind of
insight and artistry that will do justice to the power which this
myth continues to have despite McMurtry's best efforts at flog-
ging a thriving horse. If all of the Texas novels are so damn bad,
then it's clear that the subject has not been exhausted. What I
would like to see is not another *Horseman, Pass By* or *Leaving
Cheyenne*—which McMurtry assures us he has no intention of
writing—but an older, wiser, better-educated, more worldly,
more skillful Larry McMurtry graduated from these first-rate
accounts of the remnants of the frontier spirit to a great novel
on the same themes. He's as capable as anyone of doing for
the Texas frontier tradition what Faulkner did for the South.

I spend as much time as the next liberated Texan telling Yankees and Texans that such and such a view about Texas is
totally wrong, but, in the end, it is not wrong that others and
we ourselves should expect certain things of Texans just because they're Texans. No one is just a person, and Texans especially. That doesn't mean we have to be anything anyone
wants us to be: it means that we reject all of the counterfeit
myths which have been forced upon us and which we have

forced upon ourselves; but, on the other hand, it also means that if the shoe fits our history and the spirit of our history, then we had better figure out how to get our foot into it. Living up to the right idea of being a Texan is perhaps more of an issue for Texans living north of the Red River, but the fight to determine what the right idea is—which is a never-ending struggle—is one which deserves the utmost dedication from anyone who calls himself a Texan, and especially from those who haven't left. As McMurtry duly notes, of late Texans have cooperated quite gleefully in a good many schemes to push off spurious, superficial Texas myths on an unsuspecting world solely for the sake of some of that worthless green stuff. In light of the most recent epidemic of Texas fever, it seems particularly urgent that Texans ask themselves what it is they are supposed to be and what it is that those who want to be like Texans are supposed to imitate. If we spent a little more time reading some of our better writers and a lot more time asking ourselves who we are, we would still wear boots and Stetsons and drink Lone Star, but maybe we'd think twice about letting John Travolta cross the state line, or about putting out $12.95 for a string of five hundred one-liners pretending to be a novel by Dan Jenkins, or about accepting the Dallas Cowboy cheerleaders as models of Texas womanhood, to choose a few convenient examples. We wouldn't abandon the symbols of the frontier tradition, but we would demand a deeper, more reflective rendition of those symbols than the czars of Madison Avenue have been willing to give us.

Not too long after I met him, my Irish friend who had given me a way to raise some of these questions left Annapolis to go back to New Mexico. As he put it, after stumbling around through a bit of everything for his first forty years, he was going to spend the rest of his life trying to save the West.

"That's an honorable thing to do, isn't it?" he asked the day before he left.

"It sure as hell is," I said, "but leave me a little to save when I get there."

A few weeks later, he was saving New Mexico; and there I was, sitting in Annapolis, Maryland, reading Frederick Law Olmsted's 1857 *A Journey through Texas,* which for some reason, I know not why, had been sent to me by a Santa Fe bookstore—and thinking a lot about how I wanted to be in Texas when I died, and how I'd die if I wasn't there soon.

A "SOUTHERN RENAISSANCE" FOR TEXAS LETTERS

José E. Limón

> I read, much of the night,
> and go south in the winter.
> —T. S. Eliot

> . . . Home to Texas, our Texas
> That slice of hell, heaven
> Purgatory and land of our Fathers.
> —Rolando Hinojosa

The foremost of the few critics of "Texas literature" has come to believe that there is no such worthy thing. Larry McMurtry started out on his path to judgment with his 1968 essay "Southwestern Literature?" which really dealt substantially only with Texas literature defined as the books "native in the most obvious sense: set here, centered here, and for the most part, written here." (McMurtry defines literature as not only fictive writing but history, social analysis, and the essay; I too am speaking of literature in this broader sense.) Most of these Texas books were also contemporary, for, critically speaking, McMurtry saw "no point in going back beyond the thirties." Some thirteen years later he decided fully to answer the question in his title with a new essay whose subtitle explicitly tells the whole story.

The first version of this essay was delivered as an address at the Texas Literary Tradition symposium held in Austin in 1983 as part of the University of Texas's centennial celebration. A later version was published in the 28 October 1983 issue of the *Texas Observer*. That essay is reprinted here with minor additions and changes.

In "Ever a Bridegroom: Reflections on the Failure of Texas Literature," McMurtry arrives finally at a harsh judgment. The entire enterprise has been largely an exercise in literary failure from its start with Webb, Dobie, and Bedichek to the present-day efforts of their literary sons and daughters. There is more judgment than explanation in McMurtry's account, but he seems to find at least two major reasons for this failure: a lazy overindulgence in a Texas version of the pastoral and a related apparent reluctance on the part of Texas writers to read broadly and deeply. These two factors come together in a disastrous mix, producing "a limited, shallow, self-repetitious literature" dealing with "homefolks, the old folks, cowboys, or the small town," a literature "disgracefully insular and uninformed." Texas has a literary culture, but one more akin to a biologist's sense of that term, for in McMurtry's estimation, this culture has become "a pond full of self-satisfied frogs."

There is an old Mexican saying, "Silencio ranas, que va a cantar el sapo" (Be silent, frogs, the toad is about to sing). Yet even as I inject my voice into this discussion, it is not really to dispute McMurtry's critical claim, which, frankly, I endorse, albeit with an endorsement based on a more limited knowledge of the subject. Rather, I want to explore the possible reasons for this failure from a cultural anthropologist's perspective; I also want to point to one Texas regional/ethnic area not included in McMurtry's discussion, an area that might be an exception to his general indictment.

Let me begin with McMurtry's notion of the "here," for he suggests that it is the Texas writer's obsession with the rural Texas sense of time and place that vitiates this literature. Two questions emerge. First, is a concern for the "here" really the source of the problem, and second, is a significant literature of the "here" possible? I submit that McMurtry has made a too simple association between the "here" and bad literature, that the two are not necessarily correlated.

Another American region with a distinctive literary identity might provide a useful comparison. I refer to the South, and specifically what scholars call the "Southern Renaissance"—that great flowering of literature between the two World Wars that included Faulkner, Wolfe, Warren, Welty, Tate, and Ransom. In *The Faraway Country: Writers of the Modern South* (1963) Louis D. Rubin, Jr., has this to say about that period and its literature: "A time and a place have produced a body of distinguished writing. No one would think to explain the nature of that distinction merely by examining the time and the place. . . ." However, he cannot finally deny time and place—a sense of the "here"—for, while great art is in one sense transcendent,

> even so, when one looks at William Faulkner and his contemporaries, observes their sudden arrival on the literary scene when before them there was very little, notices the many similarities in the way they use language, the way they write about people, the kind of life that interests them, one is convinced that literature grows out of a culture, and that theirs has grown out of the twentieth-century South, and has its roots in Southern history and life.

Another perceptive student of the South has carried further what Rubin implies about Southern history and culture and its connection to literature. In *Consciousness and Change* (1975), the anthropologist James L. Peacock argues that many factors—the South's intense concern with the past, with kinship, hierarchy, race, and most fundamentally with a sharp insider/outsider distinction vis-à-vis the North—together have provided the nutritive matrix for a great literature as gifted Southern writers have responded with their individual talents to the interplay of this tradition and to a period of social change.

If these sorts of cultural concerns—this sense of the intense "here" and major social change—do have some responsibility for the enlargement of literature and intellect, at least in the United States, then we may wish to reconsider the Texas literary effort and ask why it failed, and has continued to fail, although, at first glance, this same anthropology of literature might seem to hold for Texas as well.

It seems to me that to the extent that history and society are responsible for the creation of literature, the general Texas experience has simply not been intense enough in comparison with that of the South—not enough group sense or sense of history, kinship, hierarchy, and race—so that when change came to Texas at the end of the nineteenth century and into the twentieth, it was gradual; the nurturing crisis, therefore, was insufficiently intense. We must not forget that we are talking about slightly less than one hundred years from the time that the first English-speaking Texans appeared in this area to the beginnings of Texas literature. Not long, as history and society go. This was a relatively mobile, open, and geographically dispersed society, from the first English-speaking illegal aliens who flooded the area in the Mexican period to today's unemployed seeking the Sunbelt. Such mobility might not make for a group beset with intense and enduring concerns for kinship, hierarchy, race, and religion. These concerns were present, as they are in most societies; they simply may not have been particularly intense or salient.

To be sure, Indians, Mexicans, and blacks were possible foils for the development of a Texas racial consciousness, but these were small in number and either quickly exterminated or pushed to the margins of white society. They could never become a haunting, stimulating influence in the development of a Texas literature comparable to the black presence in Southern fiction or the formal negation of that presence in Southern poetics. Only the Mexicans come close, particularly in the work of Webb and Dobie. In our time, non-Texans have become the primary outsider reference group for the creation of an "insider" mentality, but nothing, of course, comparable to the Southerner's consciousness of the alien North.

In short, if the particular features of Southern history and culture explain anything about their significant literature of the "here," we can sense why a great Texas literature could not be, and why McMurtry is right, even while his explanation is limited. In spite of all its real and significant differences from other states, Texas has simply not furnished sufficient cultural metaphorical depth for its writers. Certainly enough dramatic history happened here to make for literary stimulation—but not enough to provide the intense sociological conditions that could be sharply exploited by talented writers.

We come to the question of individual talents. As noted earlier, McMurtry believes that most Texas writers are intellectually ill-prepared for their task. For McMurtry (and I can only agree):

> Writing is nourished by reading—broad, curious, sustained reading; it flows from a profound alertness, fine-tuned both by literature and life. Perhaps we have not yet sloughed off the frontier notion that reading is idle or sissified. At the moment our books are protein-deficient, though the protein is there to be had, in other literatures. Until we have better readers it is most unlikely that we will have better writers.

We can easily see why books might not have been central in nineteenth-century Texas life, but I, for one, am at a loss to explain why this condition should continue to prevail among Texas writers. The real problem, I suspect, is not the lack of well-read Texas intellectuals and potential writers, but their lack of interest in Texas. Texas may be simply an insufficiently compelling literary resource which, by default, goes to minds generally of a second order. The real question is not why

Texas writers fail to read, but why the best Texas minds take
their intellectual and artistic energies to cultural domains other
than Texas.

Allow me to speculate a bit. Had the conditions of long
tradition, intense social change, and interested first-rate minds
prevailed in Texas, it is possible that we might have seen a
flowering of literature and intellectual life somewhat like that
of the South—a literary culture with the concreteness of the
"here" but with a larger, deeper exploration of the human
condition everywhere. There might have developed, therefore, a successful Texas literature and not the failure generated
by less favorable conditions. The "here" as such is not the
problem; it is the lack of historical, cultural, and intellectual
prerequisites for the significant use of the "here."

Yet it seems to me that there is at least a possibility for
such a Texas literary/intellectual culture of the "here," one
which to some degree might resemble that of the Southern
Renaissance. I refer to a group not included in McMurtry's
discussion and indictment: that is, Texas Mexicans, with their
historical and cultural predominance in their own "South"—
the southern part of Texas, including San Antonio (or at least
that city's southwestern quadrant). From these people another
limited American literary "Southern Renaissance" may be
emerging, although such a formation is still in its early stages.
It is a discourse which already includes, among others, the fiction of Rolando Hinojosa and Tomás Rivera, the urban San
Antonio poetry of Carmen Tafolla, the poetics of Gloria Anzal-
dúa, the literary criticism of Ramón Saldívar, Juan Rodriguez,
and Soñia Saldívar-Hull, and the socio-historical analyses of
Arnoldo de León, Emilio Zamora, Victor Nelson-Cisneros,
and David Montejano. At the moral and intellectual center of
this emergent culture, like some combined John Crowe Ransom, Howard Odum, and C. Vann Woodward, is the figure of
Américo Paredes, whose work informs and whose presence
guides this developing discourse.

This comparison with the South may begin with history. As Ricardo Romo has noted, one could argue that the first European literature native to Texas soil took the form of Cabeza de Vaca's fantastic reports from his travels "here" in the sixteenth century. In his essay "This Writer's Sense of Place," Rolando Hinojosa reintroduces us to a more recent, relevant history, one that most of us first learned from Américo Paredes's classic "*With His Pistol in His Hand*": *A Border Ballad and Its Hero* (1958)—the work that began this new emergence of Texas Mexican letters. Both Hinojosa and Paredes tell us of the arrival of their ancestors in South Texas as part of the mid-eighteenth-century settlement of the area that occurred even as Georgia, the last of the English colonies, was being founded. Texas Mexicans, therefore, have a long history as a unified, settled group occupying one distinctive geographical area. When change began to come to this group in the mid-nineteenth century, it did so against the grain of long tradition which had nurtured a distinctive culture.

Hinojosa's account and that of Paredes also reveal a Texas Mexican society intensely concerned with cultural themes not unlike those of the South. Here too geographical *place* is important for self- and group definition. There is a keen awareness of social hierarchy, a sharp articulation of patriarchy, intense patterns of kinship.

We also find in both accounts the historical and continuing problem of race, which has haunted the Southern imagination, but in South Texas there is a complex difference. In one sense Texas Mexicans, like Southern blacks, were the victims of racial violence and outright segregationist practices, the latter continuing well into our time. Unlike blacks, however, Texas Mexicans did not suffer slavery and discontinuity from their homeland; thus, they were more like Southern whites in relation to the North. Here we may have the most fundamental parallel to the American South. As Hinojosa notes, South Texas *was* Mexican, and thus Texas Mexicans have operated

under a historically derived insider/outsider distinction between those who were from *here* and those largely English-
speaking outsiders who, like so many "Yankees," began to
enter and dominate the area as the nineteenth century became
the twentieth. Much of the literature of the Southern Renaissance can be read as symbolic response to the Northern presence in the Southern way of life. Similarly, Texas Mexicans
had their "Northerners," and, as Paredes has shown us, they
were called *fuereños* and *gringos* (foreigners), and the very old
people of South Texas still speak of the country beyond the
Nueces as *el norte.*

This unwelcome appearance of the Northern outsiders
brings us to the theme of intense social change which has occupied such a prominent place in Southern history. More like
the Southerners and less like their fellow Anglo Texans, South
Texas Mexicans experienced severe social disruption, which
spawned different forms of class and cultural rebellion and re-
sistance. And it produced, with decidedly mixed blessings, the
slow pressures of long-term acculturation.

Social change also came from the other side of the Rio
Grande as a result of the chaos of the Mexican Revolution of
1910 and its aftermath. *That* was a war, in comparison to the
small affair of 1836. Thousands of impoverished refugees
crossed the river to join their cultural kinsmen in South Texas,
and, as Romo has shown us, this increased migration in turn
produced the phenomenon of urbanization as Mexicans found
their way to San Antonio, Houston, and Corpus Christi.

Finally and most importantly, this entire process of intense social change has been coming to a climax in the last ten
to fifteen years. Texas Mexicans now are in a position analo-
gous to that of the South between the two World Wars as tradition meets the most far-reaching social change, including
the potential loss of tradition itself. Texas Mexicans, in coming
to terms with an intense cultural past and therefore a greater
cultural threat in the present, appear to be responding, as did

Southerners, with a rich array of symbolic forms, not only literary but critical, historical, and sociological.

Another important element which must be added to this formative mix of traditional and social change is the role of learning and intellect. As McMurtry has noted, the Anglo-Texan literary tradition has not been particularly blessed with either of these, but Texas Mexicans may be in a better position in this regard. Paredes has pointed to this community's long tradition of folkloric literature, as well as an extensive written literary tradition, principally in the medium of local Spanish-language newspapers. Those writers and intellectuals who are beginning to give us the first impressions of the new Texas Mexican renaissance are drawing upon and reexamining these two traditions.

There is also a third source of learning, and herein we find a bit of irony. This Texas Mexican literary-intellectual community is a product of the institutions of higher education created by Anglo Texans, and several are now faculty members at these institutions. (Indeed, this new artistic and intellectual concern with southern Texas is being articulated principally at or through the University of Texas at Austin. Although South Texas Mexican faculty at California institutions, such as José Saldívar and the present writer at the University of California at Santa Cruz, are also participants in this emergence, South Texas Mexicans generally seem to have found both their Vanderbilt and their Chapel Hill at UT.) As such, these writers and intellectuals have a large and firm acquaintance with world letters and learning. It is an acquaintance of some intensity. As Frantz Fanon noted some years ago, the peculiar marginality which is the condition of "native intellectuals" leads them to feast

greedily upon Western culture. Like adopted children who only stop investigating the new family framework at the moment when a minimum nucleus of security crystallizes in their psyche, the native intellectual will try to make European culture his own. He will not be content to get to know Rabelais and Diderot, Shakespeare and Edgar Allan Poe; he will bind them to his intelligence as closely as possible. . . .

No one can say with any certainty how significant this "Southern Renaissance" for Texas letters will be. The writing continues; its merit will be decided in time, although already, for this critic anyway, it shows promise. According to McMurtry, Texas literature needs all the help it can get, but Texas, he and others seem to forget, does not stop at the Nueces; Anglo Texans saw to that in the nineteenth century. The intriguing paradox is that, like the Northern invasion of the South, this historical process of contact and domination of South Texas may have produced the much needed replenishment and amplification of what it means to say "Texas literature."

WHAT DOES IT TAKE
TO BE A TEXAS WRITER?

Clay Reynolds

In the past several years a virtual stampede of books by Texans about Texas has thundered onto the market, spurred no doubt by the now-passed Sesquicentennial. The works of such previously little-known writers as Elmer Kelton, Lon Tinkle, Benjamin Capps, and John Graves have emerged in shiny new and expensive paperback editions to take their places beside the somewhat more celebrated names of J. Frank Dobie, Larry L. King, Dan Jenkins, and Texas's most prominent native son Larry McMurtry. Even T. R. Fehrenbach's voluminous history of the state, *Lone Star,* has been reclaimed from the "super discount" shelves and put out front in most bookstores next to the expensive and flagrantly overwritten opus by James Michener. Texas writing, in fact, is a hot item from coast to coast and abroad as well.

From a Texan's point of view, this state of literary affairs is both natural and unremarkable. After all, as any Texan knows from birth, the state is fascinating in its variety, its history, its absolute refusal to be identified easily, to be compart-

---

This essay, in various versions, was presented as an address on several occasions during 1986 and 1987.

69

mentalized neatly; and, not incidentally, it's an enormous place with millions of diverse people and attitudes which, paradoxically, lends itself as much to stereotyping as it reserves its seemingly infinite capacity to surprise. It is, in short, a writer's paradise, a land of endless subject matter and sources for plot and character in both the state's rich history and in the contemporary, continuously unfolding saga that identifies—or perhaps fails to identify— the place and its people.

But some years ago, before the Sesquicentennial was much more than a gleam in the collective eye of the state's Chamber of Commerce presidents, a controversy over what it takes to be a Texas native—particularly a Texas native writer—was already turbulently seething, and the recent surge of Texas literature in the bookstores has done little but add more mesquite to the argument's fires.

In a way, the groups resemble serious players in what amounts to a low-stakes poker game. After all, only a handful of writers, Texan or otherwise, become rich, and with the exception of Faulkner, none has become famous solely by identifying himself with a single state. Even Faulkner is never characterized first and foremost as a "Mississippi writer." But in Texas, regardless of what there might be to gain by winning, the game is played with quiet determination, each group sternly playing out the hand it is dealt, and each relying on bluff, brag, and bet to drive the others away from the table of Texas letters in, they hope, impoverished disgrace.

One hand is held by the group of writers who ordinarily live and flourish in the "Austin–San Antonio Corridor" and spread out liberally (no pun intended) through the Hill Country. Some of the more earthy types have developed "colonies" in such unlikely locations as south of downtown San Antonio and in some roach-infested hovels and huts up and down the Guadalupe River, where they await fame and fortune as authors and poets while earning dubious livings renting innertubes and canoes to tourists. It's difficult to name names in this group, for it is amorphous and barely gets along with itself, and the membership runs from housewife-yuppie to latter-day hippie and tends to change with the seasons; however, its more successful members often find their work printed on the slick pages of *Texas Monthly* even if they themselves have removed to Taos or Santa Fe, where they carry on the battle for "Texas Writing for Texas Writers" from the comparative comfort of adobe walls.

Holding another hand—and at some distance both ideologically and geographically from the "Corridor" writers and their attendant presses and publications, which tend to bloom and die without ever taking permanent root—is a group one might dub the "New York–Texas Elite." From all reports, these writers live in posh East Side apartment houses or fashionably shabby walk-ups in Soho, where they hide from the Yankeefied evils of the Big Apple while they generate book after screenplay after novel about the Texas they left, and from where they keep in close touch with their agents and brokers. Such notables as Horton Foote, Jay Presson Allen, and, from time to time, Dan Jenkins and Larry L. King are among the celebrities in this group. The less well-known and mostly yet-to-be-discovered, it is rumored, repair regularly to Manhattan's Lone Star Café to munch chicken-fried steak and quaff longneck beers while they try to recreate a Texas ambiance and nostalgic frame of mind as they watch Kinky Friedman clown and cavort and caricature their home state.

The chief difference between the "Corridor" and the "New York–Texas" writers, however, is that some of the latter are nationally successful and write best-sellers and are Oscar and Tony winners, and the rest are at least in a position to meet and know them and, one imagines, garner favors from them; while the former aren't, don't, and by virtue of their "Corridor" isolation, can't. Hence, enmity between them is as unavoidable as it is understandable. With the addition of other players and their hands, however, the game becomes more complicated as the odds shift and the ante rises.

In Houston, for example, such writers as Edward Hirsch, Max Apple, and Phillip Lopate, among other poets and novelists, have abandoned New York and Chicago and Philadelphia and taken up residence and lucrative positions with the city's public and private universities. These writers are not Texan, either by birthright or in the subject matter of the bulk of their works; they do, however, reside in Texas, and their ranks are swelled by genuine Texans—by birth at least—such as Donald Barthelme, who has spent most of his creative energy in looking outside Texas for subject matter and most of his career, it seems, in ignoring his Gulf Coast roots, at least until it became fashionable to be Texan. These writers are a constant cause of envious outpourings of both vitriol and grudging admiration from the "Corridor" and the "New York–Texas" writers alike. The "Corridor" writers hate them for their literary prowess and recognized artistic success; the "New York–Texas Elite" hates them because they have found a way to live in Texas and make a fairly good living at their writing, even though they have no natural right to be west of the Trinity at all. The very idea of these Yankee-accented literati stomping around Texas in their hushpuppies and tweed jackets is enough to set any member of either group's teeth on edge—but then there are other positions to consider.

A fourth hand is played out by those writers who have, for one reason or another, only a narrow claim to being Texans at all. Some of this group are natives, by birth at least, but they have relocated, temporarily or permanently, elsewhere, and only a portion of their work, if any at all, concerns the Lone Star State. James Crumley, Teresa Kennedy, John Irsfeld, Andrew Hudgins, Rosalind Wright, and, more recently, Tracy Daugherty can be counted among this group working and publishing in comfortable anonymity in such diverse places as Oregon, Montana, New York State, and Ohio. And other notables, non-Texans by any definition at all, such as James Michener or Clark Howard, can be included here by virtue of their subject matter if not their residence. The success of books like Michener's *Texas*—to say nothing of the fortune its author made by visiting the state for a few months and then misrepresenting and stereotyping Texas with historical and geographic errors added for good measure—creates rancor. And the ill feeling is in no way ameliorated by such works as Don Graham's *Texas: A Literary Portrait,* a recent study of Texas as it is represented in literature. Graham includes but a handful of native Texans, past or present, in the thirty or so writers he examines.

The "Displaced Texans," of course, pay no attention whatever to the controversy about what it might take to be a Texas writer and probably couldn't care less about the issue. For the most part they are being quietly—or in Michener's case, loudly—successful at what they do, and where they were born or where they live is only of concern to them insofar as it affects book sales in the Lone Star State. Michener doesn't even have to worry about that. But the very existence of a group of writers who are identified as "Texas writers" even though the individuals therein don't make the claim themselves creates a problem for the other groups, and their recognition and literary success invite comments bordering on slander. After all, like the "New York–Texas Elite," they raise the stakes with every success they enjoy, literarily or financially.

As any Texan knows, stud poker requires a minimum of five hands to make the odds interesting, but in Texas writing, the fifth hand is so weak and disorganized that it hardly exists at all. Writers such as Winston Estes, the often forgotten Robert Flynn, Marshall Terry, Rolando Hinojosa, Benjamin Capps, and poet Walter McDonald—to name only a few of possibly a hundred or more—have been steadily publishing

for years, yet their fellow players in the game of Texas literature frequently deal them out. Like the "Corridor" group,
they are difficult to name. They are so obscurely known in
Texas—or anywhere else—that they often don't even know
each other, and in spite of their publications, they are almost
never included in either discussion or argument about Texas
writing. Occasionally one of them will hold another hand for a
while, by virtue of a successful book or a sudden shift to a
regional press, but all in all, these writers are so regularly forgotten in discussions of Texas literature that they may as well
be called the "Outside Insiders."

And then there is Larry McMurtry. He seems to play a
hand all by himself. Perhaps it is well that he does, for big as it
is, there just might not be room enough in this state for more
than one "Famous Native Son" writer. With the receipt of the
Pulitzer Prize, McMurtry seems to have righteously earned his
position as a one-man category. He is most definitely a Texas
writer, but since few if any of the authors holding any of the
other hands I've described—even those in New York and
Houston—have much chance of betting into him, the question of what it takes to be a typical "Texas writer" remains.

In his notorious 1981 essay in the *Texas Observer*, "Ever a
Bridegroom: Reflections on the Failure of Texas Literature,"
perhaps the very shot that opened this literary battle in the
state, McMurtry states that "Texas literature . . . is disgracefully insular and uninformed. . . . most Texas writers work for
a lifetime without receiving a single paragraph of intent criticism, and if they should get one now and then it will usually
come from out of state. Anything resembling a tough-minded
discussion of Texas books by a Texan is thought to be unneighborly." He goes on to assert that "only those born and
raised in Texas have the dubious honor of literary citizenship"; and he charges, "It is ironic that Texans, known the
world over for being big liars, still can't lie well enough to
write interesting novels. . . ." His essay (which extols the

work of John Graves and Donald Barthelme, among others, and despairs of Preston Jones and Larry L. King and anyone else who has tried to "return to his roots" and write about the land, the past, and the cultural heritage of the Old West with anything like a romantic eye or an attempt to find culture in the vulgar, the earthy, or the marginally obscene existence of small-town, rural Texas life) calls for a turning away from the provincial, the idealization of the mundane, and a looking outward for truths which, McMurtry asserts, cannot be found in the traditional myths of Texas proper.

McMurtry's attack on Texas writing and writers was pointed, and even his disclaimer that his intention was to shock—"I've concluded that nothing short of insult moves people in Texas"—did little to soften the blow. It was soon answered from such "Corridor" sources as *Texas Monthly,* where Gary Cartwright accused McMurtry of being an imposter as a Texan and suggested that he was the illegitimate son of Noel Coward and Aimee Semple McPherson. A flood of protest occupied the editors of the *Observer* for months. The battle was on, and it continues to this day even though the tactics have changed.

In his essay, McMurtry refuses to play the game. Instead, he singles out about three dozen individual writers for comment and either praise or complaint. He ranges widely in his sweeping survey of Texas letters, taking in such notable authors as Walter Prescott Webb and extending his examination to such contemporary writers as Billy Lee Brammer, Terry Southern, and John Graves. He forgives Katherine Anne Porter for being a Texan who didn't write much about Texas because what she did write was, somehow, "literary," and he cavils about the critical acclaim of his own first books and of other "cowboy" novels set in modern times. Such praise, he suggests, was misdirected and overstated and overly taken in by his youthful romanticization of Texas's frontier heritage. "Horses," he writes, "routinely live eighteen years, but books don't. It is quite possible that no book written in Texas in the last two or three decades will still seem worth reading eighteen years hence." He concludes by calling for books about "transition," about Houston and Dallas, about the changing face and times in the state, and he names the poet Vassar Miller the only Texas writer worthy of unqualified admiration.

To a certain extent, one can sympathize with McMurtry's position. After a huge success with what he apparently would call "modern cowboy novels"—*Horseman, Pass By* and *The Last Picture Show*—he faced the prospect of obscurity as his own "transitional" novels—*Moving On, All My Friends Are Going to Be Strangers,* and even his recent story of a "cowboy on the move," *Cadillac Jack*—failed to rise to the occasion and sustain his position as the unofficial spokesman for Texas letters, at least among Texans. For a while, he wore a tee shirt that was emblazoned with the self-parodying slogan "Minor Regional Novelist." In 1981, in fact, long before the cinema success of *Terms of Endearment,* whispers could be heard in critical circles about the "moving on" of Larry McMurtry himself as a Texas writer, since he had abandoned the state, not for New York or even for Hollywood, but for the comfortable anonymity of a D.C.–area bookstore. But now, since the film version of *Terms of Endearment* has once again placed him in the literary limelight, a triumph followed closely by the success of *Lonesome Dove,* a novel that does precisely what he condemns in his 1981 assessment of Texas literature, one has to wonder about his criteria and complaints about what it takes to be a Texas writer. Since winning the Pulitzer, in fact, McMurtry has returned to a ranch near Archer City, has published *Texasville*—a novel that returns not only to contemporary rural Texas but also to the setting and characters of *The Last Picture Show*—and has described himself with a wonderfully rustic metaphor by saying that he is a herder of words. Alas, McMurtry doesn't seem to know what it takes to be a

"Texas writer" either; or at least he didn't in 1981, and he seems to be striving now to live up to someone else's idea.

Last February, I became, officially, a "Texas writer." It was quite by accident. I just happened to live in Texas at the time my book, *The Vigil,* was accepted for publication. But I did set this first novel in Texas, as well as my second, *Agatite,* and the next two, or three, will also have Texas backgrounds, for Texas is where I was born and reared, and Texas is what I know best. Somehow writing about New York or Colorado or Florida never occurred to me. Still, when *The Vigil* was first accepted in early 1985, I informed my editor that I wanted to avoid the stigma of being called a "Texas writer." I didn't feel much like one, and I certainly had no intention of carrying the label around with me. I hadn't counted on the Sesquicentennial, though, and before I really knew it, I was caught up in the hype and rather enjoying the distinction.

Shortly after *The Vigil* appeared, David Bowen, a New Yorker now displaced to San Antonio and publisher of Corona Press, asked me why I had published with a New York press instead of a regionally based company. My initial reaction was to say that I doubted a regional press would have considered my work. After all, I had tried without any success whatever to penetrate the "Corridor" group throughout my college and graduate school years, and the rejection slips from their presses and little magazines—especially the "flagship" publication, *Texas Monthly* itself—made quite a compost heap in my desk drawer. But the truly honest answer to his question was that I never thought of it. It's one thing to send off a poem or short story with a regional setting to a regional press, but novels and plays go to New York for rejection. The Texas League is all very well for a midsummer night's entertainment, but the East Coast is where the "big kids" play. I realized, later, that I was making the "Corridor" group's argument for them.

As my work was reviewed around the country, I found myself called a "Texas writer" more and more frequently. Unfortunately, though, being called a Texas writer didn't make me one. I discovered in no time that the already well-established holders of hands around the green felt table of Texas letters left little room for a newcomer to sit in, and since I lived neither in Austin or Houston nor knew anyone in New York other than my agent, no one knew about me or cared enough even to bring me into the argument about whether I was a Texas writer or not. I wasn't even obscure enough to hold cards in the fifth hand, the "Outside Insiders" of Texas letters. I was playing solitaire. Regardless of what reviewers called me, regardless of the publicity surrounding the state's birthday, I was only a Texas writer by virtue of birth, geography, and subject matter, and I still was unsure of what else it took to acquire my bonafides—if I really wanted them in the first place.

At the same time, I realized that I wasn't entirely sure of just who the Texas authors actually were. I felt terribly ignorant of other Texas literature, and I decided that if I ever expected to be asked to play, I had better learn who else was around the table. Except for J. Frank Dobie, Larry McMurtry, Robert Flynn, Preston Jones (who was properly New Mexican, not Texan), Horton Foote, and possibly Larry L. King and Dan Jenkins, I knew next to nothing about native Texas literature. Therefore, I took McMurtry's advice and began reading.

I began with A. C. Greene's list of the fifty best (in his opinion) Texas books, and I supplemented it with McMurtry's discussion in the 1981 article. I already knew Katherine Anne Porter's work, of course, and I was familiar with Barthelme and a few of the transplanted Texas writers, and then I turned to Elmer Kelton and Benjamin Capps, John Graves and Winston Estes, a writer who, ironically, came from my own hometown but whom I had never had the time or interest to read before. Others whose work had somehow slipped my notice over the years were conveniently finding themselves reprinted during this 150th birthday celebration, and so my home library's shelves began to swell with my own new collection of Texana.

At this point, I'm still reading, and there are hundreds of books and authors to go—well, maybe dozens—but the result to date has been a delightful discovery of a rich literary tradition that is, I believe, unique as Texas is unique. The cowboy myths and legends, the Spanish and Mexican history, the Indians and soldiers and buffalo hunters that crisscrossed the state during the eighteenth and nineteenth centuries, the politics of the twentieth century, real estate, oil, the military, the medicine, the murderers—all of it seemed to coalesce into as strong a regional identity as I had ever been able to find, even in Carson McCullers or William Faulkner, Hamlin Garland or Sherwood Anderson. Such a euphoric discovery was undiminished by McMurtry's caveat that too many Texas writers turn to such traditional subjects and therefore betray their literary sensibilities. And I dismissed his denigration of his first two major successes as juvenile pratings in light of his own "return to the land" and the well-established myths of Texas's frontier past in *Lonesome Dove*.

My reading introduced me to the genuine, heartfelt writing of Elmer Kelton, whose subjects—cowboys, ranchers, cavalrymen, Indians—are treated with a craftsmanship and an art that is surely worthy of the same words of praise McMurtry afforded Vassar Miller's work. Of her poetry he said, "There is definitely a there there: hard-won, high, intelligent, felt, finished, profound." The same can be said of Kelton's *The Time It Never Rained, The Day the Cowboys Quit,* and most certainly of *The Wolf and the Buffalo.* And it could be said of others' works as well, works which seemed to escape McMurtry's notice in 1981.

One writer of whom it cannot be said, of course, is James

Michener, whose latest literary indiscretion, *Texas,* has been
selling like mesquite-smoked barbecue both in Texas and elsewhere. I waded through the entire twelve hundred pages of
Michener's parody of a novel, and when I concluded it, I found
satisfaction only in the book's incredible, ponderous length:
few readers would have either the time or the inclination to
finish it and would, therefore, be spared the author's almost
absurd misconceptions and errors, poor style, and weak char-
acterization. One thing McMurtry and I and the others around
the green felt table of Texas letters would have to agree on is
that it takes more than money and an automatic best-seller to
make an author a Texas writer.

But when I looked at my own fiction and discovered
sheriffs, ranchers, farmers, and petty politicians, in short a collection of what Preston Jones called "sag-bellied bores," pop-
ulating my imaginary small town, I realized that I had, for
better or worse, subscribed to the same spirit that McMurtry
and many of the "New York–Texas Elite" had condemned or,
like Dan Jenkins and Larry L. King, had laughed at: the spirit
of provinciality. But did that make me, again, for better or
worse, a "Texas writer"? Not really.

Tom Pilkington, arguably one of the most knowledge-
able critics and commentators on contemporary Texas fiction,
recently defined a "Texas writer" as a writer who was born in
and has lived in Texas most of his or her life and, he added
almost quietly, who writes about Texas. I fit that category, as
do a great number of the writers who make claim to the title,
but that doesn't necessarily turn the trick either. I might don a
leather jacket, a bolo tie, and boots made from four kinds of
hand-chewed leather, wear a Stetson and drive a Suburban,
say "Haw-yew" and wash hot jalapeños down with Shiner
beer, name my son for a Texas cowboy uncle and my dog for a
notorious San Antonio prostitute, root for the Longhorns, the
Astros, and the Dallas Cowboys, attend rodeos, invest in oil
leases, dip snuff, talk flood, drought, hail, and twisters, cotton,

wheat, beef, oil, and the problem of the "Mescan" border, and try to convince my in-laws that a tractor pull is the greatest entertainment since Barnum and Bailey; but none of that would make me any more of a Texas writer than would selling incense and hand-crafted jewelry on "the Drag" in Austin make me an artist. It might, however, get me a role in the television movie of Michener's book. By examining my own writing in the cold, unforgiving criticism of McMurtry's complaint, I came to realize that it takes something more than merely affecting a style to be a part of the region one writes about. And it takes more than simply recreating Texans as they appear either to me or to outsiders. It takes a sense of that region and those people as well. The acquisition of that sense is not restricted to a person's birthplace or where he or she chooses to live. In the simplest terms, to be a Texas writer—or a writer from anyplace else—an author has to come to know Texas—or that anyplace else—and to respond to it with an understanding that goes deeper than anything research teams or a quick overview of the land and a few handshakes can accomplish.

In a March 24, 1986, *New York Times* article concerning the celebration of the fiftieth anniversary of the Texas Institute of Letters—the one organization that has tried more than any other to bridge the gaps and smooth out the differences between the quarreling groups of Texas writers—Stephen Harrigan, novelist and senior editor of *Texas Monthly,* Donald Barthelme, Max Apple, John Graves, A. C. Greene, and others all gathered and were cited in their unanimous defense of the quality of Texas writing, which they declared was revealed in the longevity and value of the Institute. Harrigan summed up the controversy in Texas letters by pointing out, "Fifty years ago no one could agree what it was supposed to be. . . . Now no one can agree on what it's become. But Texas has had the peculiar climate that allowed it to flourish. I don't think there could be a New Jersey Institute of Letters." To a certain extent, Harrigan's comment illustrates more of the same sort of

Texas chauvinism McMurtry—the TIL's major honoree that year—had complained of five years before. But the unanimity shown at the TIL banquet as well as the coverage by such papers as the *New York Times,* Harrigan noted, also illustrated that Texas letters was receiving important attention. "To the extent there is a public image of the TIL," he said, "it probably consists of the idea of a bunch of guys wearing pants tucked into their boots and twirling lariats. But the more the TIL is taken seriously, the more you can be sure Texas is becoming more like anyplace else."

The *Times* reporter, himself a writer for *Texas Monthly,* pointed out the fact that many of the TIL's members are not native Texans and some, like Apple and Barthelme, barely even write about the state or its traditions at all, but Harrigan and his fellow TIL members were quick to make the distinction between regionalism and provincialism, the latter being the true target of McMurtry's original complaint. To write about a place, they suggested, even a place as rich in identity as Texas, does not de facto make that author provincial any more than writing about New York makes a native New Yorker provincial, though provincial New Yorkers certainly can be. The depth and value of literature lie in its ability to reveal the depth and value of character, to understand the human condition, to create a cultural chart of a place and a people that is not restricted by historical facts and statistical analysis but somehow speaks to a universality of values and emotions that transcends place and time in its quest to define the American character. To attempt to do so much is to attempt to approach art, and whether such art involves Elmer Kelton's cowboys and Indians, Robert Flynn's old traildriver, Dan Jenkins's washed-up football players, Jane Gilmore Rushing's Future Farmers, Jane Roberts Wood's schoolmarm, Horton Foote's farm widows, Preston Jones's Knights of the White Magnolia, Dorothy Scarborough's wind, Larry L.

King's Miss Mona, or Larry McMurtry's Danny Deck and Cadillac Jack really doesn't matter. Also it doesn't matter whether the writer was born in Texas, lives in Texas, or even writes about Texas at all. Even the TIL would agree that Shakespeare, Hugo, Joyce, and Sophocles were pretty fair writers, though they never drank a Lone Star or sat in hundred-degree sunshine and watched a thunderstorm raging eighty miles away across the prairie. The important thing is that writers remain true to their subject matter and faithful to their characters and setting.

Thus, the various groups arguing over what it takes to be a Texas writer are really saying the same thing. It takes no more or less to be a Texas writer than it does to be any other kind of writer. McMurtry has returned with tremendous success to rural settings and archetypal themes drawn from the past, and his effort has gained him a Pulitzer among other kudos, even if much of *Lonesome Dove* was completed in a bookstore in Georgetown rather than in Texas. The Sesquicentennial brought national recognition to such writers as Elmer Kelton and Benjamin Capps, elevating their work from the dusty racks of the pulp Western and placing it in prominence in the nation's bookstores. And the result has been a celebration of a region and its people through the literature of its writers.

There are many stories to tell about Texas. And, like their writers, some of them will be, as Phillip Lopate has stated, "too narcissistic." They will try to impress outsiders with the multitudes of myths and reminiscences that such a place continually produces even in modern times, even outside the major traditions. But Lopate also acknowledged, "It's a big state. . . . There can't just be one myth." Dealing with those myths and the people who create them and try to live them is what makes an author a Texas writer. The Lone Star State has produced quite a number of decent writers already, some born here, some who merely have transplanted their talents from elsewhere, and some who have moved away to gain distance and objectivity as they deal with a subject that haunts them.

Tom Pilkington asserted during a conversation in 1986 that in his 1981 attack on Texas letters, McMurtry was "putting us on" by putting down those contemporary efforts to capture the mystique of Texas in celebration of the state's chauvinistic past. I tend to think Pilkington is right about that, for in *All My Friends Are Going to Be Strangers,* McMurtry describes the feeling Danny Deck has as he leaves Texas, and, in doing so, reveals his own sense of that mystique and the power of being from such a special place:

> It was strange, leaving Texas. I had no plans to leave it, and didn't know how I felt. . . . Then I really felt Texas. It was all behind me, north to south, not lying there exactly, but more like looming there over the car, not a state or a stretch of land but some giant, some genie, some god, towering over the road. I really felt it. Its vengeance might fall on me from behind. I had left without asking permission, or earning my freedom. Texas let me go, ominously quiet. It hadn't gone away. It was there behind me.

In the thoughts of his fictional author-narrator, McMurtry may come closer than anyone to defining what it takes to be a Texas writer. More than birthright, residence, or a sense of myth and tradition, the feeling of a need to stay with such a vast and varied land, with such a powerful and dominating spirit, to stay with it and tell its story seems to be the single thread that unites almost all the Texas writers who rage and fume and pretend to ignore one another. The absence of that feeling is what characterizes such books as Michener's *Texas* and Edna Ferber's *Giant* as being hopelessly myopic and erroneous and sterile. The feeling he describes is what it takes to be a Texas writer. In the past 150 years it has produced a number of good ones; with luck, there will be more to come. But for the moment, I hope all the "Texas writers" continue to feud and fuss about the question. That's grist for the literary mill in the state, and without it, I'm not sure any of us would have the right to call ourselves Texans, writers or otherwise.

REQUIEM FOR A TEXAS LADY

Celia Morris

I learned on my own—I learned the hard way—that a good old boy can be one of the meanest things in God's creation, but it took a dead woman to teach me why.

I have had the sobering pleasure of living for more than a decade now with an extraordinary Scotswoman named Frances Wright, who came to this country first in 1818, when she was twenty-three. My book about her, *Fanny Wright: Rebel in America,* was published by Harvard University Press in 1984, and was co-winner of that year's Texas Institute of Letters's Carr P. Collins Award for distinguished nonfiction. I took an unholy relish in that award: my former husband and several men whose friendship had graced my twenties and thirties had won it earlier, and during our years together, neither they nor I had ever dreamed I might aspire to the prize, much less grasp it. The experience of writing the book, because it forced me to confront the assumptions with which I had been raised—because it taught me what was wrong with being a lady—turned me in middle age into a radical.

This essay is a revised version of the keynote address delivered by Celia Morris at the Texas Women Scholars conference held at the University of Texas at Austin in the spring of 1986.

The woman who had this transforming power over me had so disturbed our national equilibrium that most people subsequently contrived to forget about her for more than a century after her death. Brought up to be a lady out of the pages of Jane Austen, Fanny Wright had turned against her own class in search of a way to make her life matter in the world. She had taken Thomas Jefferson at his literal word when he wrote, "All men are created equal," and she lived and thought on the assumption that "men" meant "women" as well. At twenty-five, she became the first woman in the United States of America to act publicly to oppose slavery: she set up a commune just outside Memphis, Tennessee, the purpose of which was to discover and to demonstrate how slaves could be responsibly educated and then freed at no great loss to those who owned them. In 1828, she became the first woman in America to speak in public to a large, secular, "promiscuous" audience of men and women, and the first to argue publicly that women were men's equals and should act as such and be treated as such in all the business of public life.

She did her most important work more than 150 years ago. And after years of studying all the evidence I could find, I concluded that Fanny Wright had been destroyed politically for three main reasons: one, for preaching equality—the equality of women and men, the equality of blacks and whites; two, for saying publicly that sexual passion was "the strongest and the noblest of the human passions"; and three, for living as though she were the equal of any man. She insisted that women and men had to work politically and culturally *together,* and *as equals,* to shape a world that had any balance or made any sense at all, and for that insistence she became the most notorious woman in Jacksonian America. I oversimplify only slightly when I say that she was politically destroyed because she took positions I now take for granted. But many people, I discovered, still find Fanny Wright unnerving. Some, in fact, find her terrifying, no doubt because the fault lines she exposed in American society remain there still.

The cogent arguments she made, along with what happened to her in this country, for instance, forced me to look hard at what had happened to me and to the women I grew up with—women who came of age in Texas in the 1950s. We had grown up believing in the American rhetoric of equality. We were influenced, however subtly, by the tradition of strong frontier women: many of us had exceedingly tough grandmothers. We were young women who worked hard. We were smart, or so we thought. We were the lucky ones.

But, as it turned out, we were not to be the equals of our male peers, nor were we expected to be. The discovery of these facts, somewhere in our middle twenties and early thirties, came to us as a terrible surprise. It is now thirty years since we turned twenty-one—Jessie Barnard's "prime time" for women—and some of us, even when we had to learn the lesson more than once, have finally fought our way to being *essentially* equal. But the fight has been terrifically hard; the outcome often by no means clear; and our good fortune, such as it has been, both precarious and deeply dependent on the resurgence of the American women's movement at the end of the 1960s.

When life and Fanny forced me to reexamine my own experience, I realized that like many of my friends, I had grown up idolizing Melanie in *Gone with the Wind,* and I knew that one did not violate with impunity an image so gentle. (I did not understand until much later that if you wanted to be Melanie you had to die young: early death was an integral part of that package.) Scarlett was too silly and too cruel, and besides, she lost Rhett Butler in the end.

Most of my friends—white women of the middle and upper-middle classes—took for granted the myth Melanie embodied about a woman's place. (When we came of age in the 1950s, we knew only one story, really, which ended, "And they lived happily ever after.") That myth seemed to take women seriously and at the same time virtually guarantee the good life. It assumed that woman's place was in the home, where anyone who deserved it would find what happiness there was in an otherwise imperfect world. It tendered women the greatest respect and gave them the most important moral and social task—the bringing up of children. They were to be protected from the ugly world of work. And everyone knew that behind a successful man was a clever woman. In the prevailing mythology, women had everything: adoration, respect, protection, and power. In return for good behavior, reasonably good looks, and the good sense to choose the right husband, life would bestow a series of joys one could feel deeply, challenges one could rise to, responsibilities one could usefully fulfill. Texas of course had no proprietary claim on that myth— the place-name can easily serve as a metaphor for a state of mind—but I want to think about it now in terms of Texas simply because that's where I knew it best.

Women who have been something other than wives and mothers have, in fact, played a large role in Texas, but that phenomenon has been a well-kept secret. I confirmed my suspicions on such matters by means of an eleven-part query I sent to about forty women who grew up here. Their ages ranged from the mid-twenties to the mid-seventies; after a great deal of sturm und drang, many are now reasonably successful professional women; and their answers demonstrated how little we know about our own past. The only one of four important political women, for instance, who came from Texas and whom most of them recognized was Ma Ferguson, about whom all but one confessed to knowing very little. Only two had read Dorothy Scarborough's *The Wind.* All of them said their educations had taught them very little about women in American history, very little about women in any of the arts, and almost nothing about women in Texas. To the questions that elicited those responses the writer Linda West Eckhardt answered most cogently for all the rest when she wrote a series of *ha ha ha*'s from the left margin of the page to the right.

I asked each to say something about what she considered distinctively "Texan" about her, and several found nothing at all. My favorite response came from Betty Dooley, who directs the research arm of the Congressional Caucus for Women's Issues on Capitol Hill and who said, "I've come to believe that the morons, thieves, and cutthroats who with their women settled Texas have passed on genetically a spirit of independence, courage, and tenacity which has given me an edge over these defeated, pessimistic, and cynical Easterners." Apart from that gift, which some of us are lucky to share, it was clear that we had been denied our own past, along with being denied the full range of models of human possibility.

In fact, if you knew Texas only through its best-known writing, you would be hard-pressed to believe that competent, adult, self-defining women exist here—women, that is, who do not define themselves essentially by their relationship to a man. Our state is known to the world, and, I fancy, often to itself, primarily by the things men do outdoors—by wars in its early days, gradually by cattle, subsequently by oil, and now by football. Its mythos is overwhelmingly masculine. Although one of my contemporaries wrote of herself as profoundly shaped by the strong women stretching back in her family, she, her sister, and daughter agreed that they had always felt somewhat cheated, or at least left out, "because we had no real feel for the Texas that everyone else seems to have: the land, cowboys, oil wells, cattle, Indians. . . . None of us feels at all affected by having lived among these legends, neither infused with them nor sentimental about them. Not much interested and not affected." But apart from admiring and sustaining the men who win at any of the games they play, or sharing in the lavish display of wealth they gain by winning, women do not play a large role in the popular Texas stories.

Since we all grow up as part of a continuum, in order to know ourselves we need to understand the traditions from which we derive. Both John Graves's *Goodbye to a River,* for instance, and Larry McMurtry's *In a Narrow Grave* are explorations of the Texas past and attempts by the authors to put themselves in some genuine, creative relation to it. Both are ultimately exercises in self-understanding. In the former, Graves writes as follows: "The provincial who cultivates only his roots is in peril, potato-like, of becoming more root than plant. The man who cuts his roots away and denies that they were ever connected with him withers into half a man. . . . It's not necessary to like being a Texan. . . . It is, I think, necessary to know in that crystal chamber of the mind where one speaks straight to oneself that one is or was that thing, and for any understanding of the human condition it's probably necessary to know a little about what the thing consists of." Like most men, Graves no doubt uses the male pronoun as a surrogate for "human," but frankly it doesn't work for me. These two are fine books, but they are by no means universal: they are men's books. I discover virtually nothing in either that helps me understand myself as a Texan or even as a human being—nor did those authors turn for self-understanding to the opposite sex: in a combined bibliography of almost fifty titles, they refer to only three books by women.

Even men otherwise distinguished for rigorous thinking incline to bemusement on the subject of women. Sigmund Freud wondered what women wanted. Larry McMurtry, whose work shows that he sees women and even, on occasion, finds one to admire, tends to think stereotypically about them, to imagine them in terms of what they do or feel in relation to a man. In his virtuoso essay, "Ever a Bridegroom," he says of John Graves, "If nature continues to stimulate him it may be because it too is elusive, feminine, never completely knowable."

In trying to come to terms with the chasm between what the Texas myth promised for women and what life has actually brought me, I decided to look over some of the novels written by Texas men who are roughly of my generation. More than one of those writers has been a good friend of mine: the world they described was the world we had shared. I have admired and liked them, and thought them honest men. They have taken it as their business to describe the society around them with intelligence, integrity, and style. Foregoing boosterism and cant, they have succeeded in part on how clearly and deeply they could see into our shared life. And when I read their work with an eye to seeing where women fit into the scheme of things, I discovered that the myth had always been a cheat.

I want to focus first on this fiction, which most literate Texans know, because I think it suggests the dimensions of our problem. Some of that fiction is good, and for much of it I am grateful. But the hard truth is that when men write about Texas, they either leave women on the peripheries, or they imagine lives any gutsy, self-respecting woman would hate to have. Reading our native sons confirmed conclusions to which I had come as I thought back on my own experience: they seemed to teach that women were not ordinarily allowed to live here as the equals of men—were not encouraged to develop and use their gifts as freely.

Among those writers, I found that Larry King was in a class of his own, and so I could talk about him separately. A reader can say of him what John Jay Chapman said of Emerson: the worst Italian opera can teach a visitor from Mars what the collected works of Emerson cannot—the fact that there are two sexes. King, too, is virtually blind to women. I may be justly accused here of hurt feelings, since in talking of the people at my former husband Willie Morris's "Ole Country Boys Party," King mentions "Robert Penn Warren, Ralph Ellison, William Styron, Tom Wicker, C. Vann Woodward, Marshall Frady, Morris, and a half-dozen others." Perhaps Larry intended that half-dozen to include the women there. As I recall, one of them had won a National Book Award, another was an accomplished journalist and writer of children's stories, still another a translator of Russian poetry. And since on those occasions I cooked, served, and then cleaned up an extraordinary amount of debris, I thought I deserved more explicit and generous mention than I got.

However, I'm a great admirer of Larry King's. One good friend of mine said to another: "Do yourself a favor sometime: get drunk with Larry King," and I've done myself that favor more than once in the past quarter-century. He's got a good ear, a keen eye, and, despite the vices he lays claim to, energy enough for ten. He's written about his daddy, racism, television, Sugar Ray Robinson, Joe Pool, Norman Mailer, Louis Armstrong, Lyndon Johnson, and Lyndon's brother Sam Houston Johnson. He's written about Oxford, Mississippi; Putnam, Texas; and Harvard. But he doesn't write about women.

True, in his novel *The One-Eyed Man* there's a woman called Roxie who's not bad. She's a gutsy woman who's lived and suffered and laughed and who bears, even in name, a suspicious resemblance to King's late wife Rosemarie. But she gets no more than twenty pages in a book that's over three hundred pages long; she isn't, that is, necessary in any way to what the book is about. She's described almost entirely in terms of her relationships with men, and one suspects that the editor said, We need some sex to make it sell.

The book is about politics by a man who was bemused, as so many were, by Lyndon Johnson. It is full of rich political experience: it puts the lie to official rhetoric about the way government works and gives us that cozy insider's sense that now we know what really juices political life. But it knows nothing about women, except that they are people who mess up men's lives and are occasionally pleasant to screw.

It would be cruel to quote though easy to find the passages that are most typical of Larry King on women. (I can't resist noting one reference to "Chick Starter [which is not a new aphrodisiac for hippie girls, but a product to feed infant chickens].") The important fact is that a writer so gifted, so experienced, so ambitious, and so primarily identified with Texas neither sees women nor describes a social world in which they matter.

It was some years ago when I first made these discoveries about Larry King and crafted a few preliminary paragraphs about his writing. When I was done, I called and read him what I had on paper. He listened with bursts of pained, angry laughter, but he was generous enough to like it. Or so he said. Subsequently he wrote *The Best Little Whorehouse in Texas*. And frankly, I've never summoned the courage to ask him whether *Whorehouse* was at least in small part a way of thumbing his nose at me, since I didn't know how to say, "Larry, that's not quite what I had in mind."

There are other writers, however—William Humphrey, Bill Brammer, Dan Jenkins, and Larry McMurtry—in whose work women do figure significantly, and I looked at those women with questions in mind. I wanted to know whether they were people with self-respect; whether they had opportunities that challenged them; whether they had daily work that mattered and satisfied. And it was not a cheering experience.

If one looked at middle-aged women, who interested me for obvious personal reasons, one found, for the most part, lives that had been made to rest on sexual relationships that had gone awry—ravaging their emotions and leaving little for them to do. Humphrey's *Home from the Hill*, for instance, gives considerable space to a woman in the midst of living according to the myth. Her name is Hannah Hunnicutt, and on dis-

covering that her husband is compulsively and notoriously
unfaithful, she decides to be an irreproachable wife, which to
her means sexually unapproachable:

> He vowed to forsake all others and he has broken his
> vow a dozen times to my knowledge, which means a
> hundred times more that I never knew of, no doubt, and a
> thousand times more in his thoughts. But let him see how
> I keep my vow! . . . Every time he breaks his will make
> me strengthen mine!

Whether or not this is simply an instance of a male writer
engaging in wishful thinking, Hannah clenches her teeth
rather than exuberantly discovering the richness of life—of
which sexuality is of course only a part. She is limited by her
own nature and by what she accepts of the code of her class
from joining in the lives of people outside her family—either
by work or by charity or by common cause. She lives for her
son:

> She had studied to keep up with the boy's interests,
> which were intense, passionate, and short-lived. . . . she
> learned to tie Boy Scout knots, memorized the Morse code,
> learned to make crystal set radios, learned the Periodic
> Table when it was a chemistry set that absorbed him.

In return for her self-sacrifice, she loses her son's love and respect; her husband loses his life (his love, if she had ever had
it, she had lost long before); and she goes mad.

Home from the Hill describes a society that forced respect-
able women to live through their children, and thereby ruined
both them and their children. Much of the book, indeed, is a
hymn to hunting: to rituals in which women have no part, to
ways men have of exploring and defining their humanity which
have nothing to teach them about their lives in relation to
women. There are, besides Hannah, other impressive women

in Humphrey's work: Ella Ordway in *The Ordways* is an example. But for all of them sexual morality is the only morality there is, and they are isolated inside the home from the occupations and pastimes the author most eagerly describes.

Two other women, both of them from McMurtry's fiction, come to mind: they are white, middle-aged, middle-class, and have had children. Lois, in *The Last Picture Show,* is one of the most attractive characters in McMurtry's work. She has got "more life than just about anybody in this town," but she has had nothing to do with all her energy. She has frightened her husband into making a good deal of money: "He's so scared of me that for twenty years he's done nothing but run around trying to find things to please me. He's never found the right things but he made a million dollars looking." Because she is rich, she has the easy social option of shocking her neighbors, but she gets no lasting satisfaction from doing that or anything else. Her frivolous daughter dismays her, and the world she lives in grossly disappoints her energies, her imagination, and her need: "life's too damn hard here. . . . The land's got too much power over you. Being rich here is a good way to go insane," she complains. "Everything's flat and empty and there's nothing to do but spend money."

Lee Duffin in *Moving On,* a stylish, brittle Easterner, is equally unhappy. Her daughters have left for college, and their absence makes her face her husband's indifference, the waning sexual attractiveness that comes with middle age (a phenomenon far more true in America than in any European country), and the emptiness of her life:

> I used to be quite a piece, I guess. All his colleagues were
> hot for me and we worked it out pretty well, but here I
> am forty-four and those of his colleagues who go in for
> that sort of thing have got to the age of screwing graduate
> students, or undergraduates if they've got the guts. . . .

nobody's made a pass at me since we moved here, including Bill. . . . If I didn't love him it wouldn't be such a
trap, but I seem to love him. I guess I'm a masochist.

She finally takes a graduate student lover, who calms her
nerves and flatters her vanity.

Apart from Molly in *Leaving Cheyenne,* virtually all the
sympathetic women McMurtry carefully observes live in various stages of unhappiness. They drink, garden, flirt, spend
money, are stoic, have affairs. But they are marking time.
None of them find deep and sustaining friendship possible
with other women; only one has serious work; and the main
difference in the way they respond to the same dilemma lies in
their resilience. Jenny Salomea, for example, in *All My Friends
Are Going to Be Strangers,* hides her sexual ignorance and fear,
and tries bravely to seduce Danny Deck:

> "I love Sally," [Danny] said. "I better give monog-
> amy a chance."
> "I took that attitude once," she said, holding out her
> champagne glass. "Now I'd rather give cunnilingus a
> chance."

In all these books there is only one woman, Eleanor
Guthrie in *Moving On,* who has had serious responsibilities
that are not domestic. She has inherited and run one of the
great Texas ranches and in doing so has had work she could
do well that absorbs and interests her. Early divorced and
childless, she stands self-sufficient, even when she flies about
the country for diversion, and even when she carries on an
affair with a rodeo champ, the notorious Sonny:

> He knew she was proud and gluttonous. He had no inter-
> est in changing her, or in marrying her. He would never
> make her better, nor she him. They could only get worse,
> more violent, more emotional, more sordid. . . . He had

been a continent, her continent, Sonny had. What she
feared was that she had come to the end of him.

She is the only woman I have discussed who can make that
kind of recognition at the end—that she can and will do without a man she has loved.

Most of these are women for whom the myth has set a
trap. It romanticized both marital love and women's work inside the home. It refused to see that women could not ade-
quately educate their children if they were ignorant of the
world for which they were preparing them. It failed to acknowledge how fragile the love between a man and a woman
can be. It failed to provide for the void children leave when
they grow up. And it discouraged women from trying to find
valuable work they could spend a lifetime learning to do well.

As for the young women in Texas fiction, the most illuminating I found was Dan Jenkins's Barbara Jane Bookman.
Because *Semi-Tough* is a comic novel about professional football, there are several reasons not to take Barbara Jane seriously, even though she gets some of the book's best lines. She
lives in a world where everybody who counts is beautiful,
rich, free, famous, perpetually young—where tears don't last,
and the end may surprise but won't sadden. Most of us don't
live in that world, and maybe that's why reading about it gives
such pleasure. But a nagging worry persists: may Jenkins, after
all, really believe in his Barbara Jane as a model of womanhood?
Because she is, in fact, a modern version of the myth.

She is a wind-up doll with an "NFL body" who presides
at orgies but screws only Shake Tiller. A fantasy of fidelity,
she's a combination of Scarlett and Melanie in modern dress—
or, rather, undress—sexy, aggressive, apparently independent,
but at the same time faithful, gentle, and kind. Or imagine
the old Bacall toughness without the langour. She's a high-
energy, wise-cracking, high-rent babe—who is also, and always has been, one of the boys.

Let's listen to the qualities Barbara Jane, Shake, and their friend Billy Clyde list for the best woman they can imagine—a "One"—for which, as they put it, "Barb herself was in the running":

> extremely gorgeous . . . never got mad at anything a man might accidentally do . . . good-natured and could laugh a lot and enjoy all kinds of people no matter how boring they were . . . was a lady at all times . . . could cook any-thing a man wanted . . . could cool out everybody else on the floor but . . . never asked to dance . . . was well-read and smart and witty but not as well-read and smart and witty as some guys she hung around with . . . highly ap-preciative of what a man said . . . stylish in the way she dressed . . . didn't particularly care about ever getting married . . . a happy drunk and never aggressive . . . en-joyed every kind of normal sexual adventure under the proper circumstances . . .

It is a great put-on in the comic tradition, a wonderful laugh at the arrogance and weakness of men, whose egos, apparently, are so fragile that women have to exist wholly in soothing re-lation to them, who seem compulsively afraid of being out-classed; who can't cope with mind, spirit, soul, or even un-ladylike behavior. The editors of *Ms.* could not have done a better parody, and Jenkins knew it was a put-on.

At the same time, Jenkins took her seriously enough, and so, I discovered to my dismay, did many of his readers, that I couldn't simply write her off as a funny lady in a funny book. In fact, she was a manipulative woman who used her body to make her fortune. And her range of possible expression and feeling was extremely narrow: invariably she took her lead from men and had no real life except in response to them. She could never need anything it wasn't polite to ask for, never hurt in a way that would be unseemly, never be un-selfish enough to trouble herself about anyone else's suffer-

ing. To see the downside of that type, you can look to Jacy, in
The Last Picture Show, whom McMurtry describes with stun-
ning hostility. Neither is a woman you'd want to imagine
grown up.

When these writers describe young women who are married and have children, they tend to be sympathetic and baffled.
Like McMurtry, Bill Brammer in *The Gay Place* is a writer who
convinces us that he can see real women and care about them.
(He was like that too: he is the only grown man who ever
made me feel maternal, and many other women responded
similarly to him.) But he is suspicious of the world in which
the myth says they ought to find happiness, and the men in his
book are dubious about women. For the most part they resemble Roy Sherwood, who "did not much like women . . .
though he thought about them most all the time. He simply
felt they were up to no good." And in *The Gay Place* most of
them are, really—so are the men. They have lost a vision of
what the good might mean, and they don't know what to do
with themselves.

When she is not out with men other than her husband,
Brammer's Andrea Christiansen plays with her two daughters:
"We invent games. We put on plays. We put dresses on the
dog and wear lipstick and paint our toenails. . . ." It isn't a
promising way for a grown woman to grow up. Becoming absorbed in the lives of their children offers women like Andrea
no hope: Brammer knows that adults must live adult lives.
But, looking around him, he apparently finds little worth pursuing, and the marriages he describes are in various stages of
decay.

Patsy Carpenter, in *Moving On,* is—unintentionally, I'm
sure—McMurtry's refutation of the myth. She is a city woman
in her early twenties who is not a bitch. Attractive and intelligent, she neither has to work to support herself nor is she
told by her culture that she ought to do so. With an aimless
husband who does not move her deeply, she is ignorant of life

but doesn't know it. Since she has done nothing and little has happened to her, she hasn't much to reflect upon. She has been betrayed by her culture's elaborate respect for a young woman's physical beauty and its insistence, until recently, on sexual ignorance.

By the time they are Patsy's age, most Texas men, as the fiction describes them, will have spent years in the active companionship of other men; they will have fought and worked and explored at least some part of their world; they will have lost their sexual innocence—if they're from small towns or the country apparently with the help of animals (which may be overrated as a sexual experience but is an experience nevertheless). They will have had to face the question of vocation and explored their talents and interests sufficiently to give them an idea what to do with themselves. The luckiest ones in McMurtry's fiction will have had an affair with an older woman and read some books.

Patsy finally breaks a bit from the vacuum of her protected life: she has a child; she discovers adultery; she reads; and she suffers with the suffering of her friends. She meets people different from any she's known and has to learn to see them. She discovers physical passion and learns to deceive. She then discovers the emptiness of mere sex and comes to rage at men who want to put her on a pedestal. She learns to recognize her own confusion:

> . . . if happiness lay in large things rather than small, in the fulfillment of major needs and adequacy to major responsibilities, then she felt lost. Honor and honesty, fidelity, responsibility, duty, love, all did less for her spirits than buying baby clothes and cooking waffles. There were days when the ability to cook a good breakfast seemed the only hope for her character.

By the time we leave her, she has become a rather reflective, independent, and resourceful woman, but she has no focus for either her sexual or her intellectual energies.

In short, I decided on the basis of the fiction written by its native sons, that the old Texas myth about women finding happiness in the home had not panned out. The two women one would judge most nearly content had broken through the strictures of propriety altogether. One of them, Molly in *Leaving Cheyenne,* had a lifelong affair with two men who were best friends; the other, Eleanor Guthrie in *Moving On,* as I mentioned earlier, ran her own ranch and indulged in an affair with a notorious rodeo rider. I concluded that the Texas literature in question either ignored women altogether, dealt with them peripherally, turned them into shrews and viragos—or it treated them affectionately and showed them at their best to be angry, frustrated, undeveloped, and confused—if sometimes honest, gutsy, and alive. One final revealing fact: the women in the novels of Texas's native sons have no politics or political vision whatever.

Many women in Texas and elsewhere surely answer to this description. Most of the women I know best do not.

Within the past few years, two more books have been published that deserve at least some further attention in this context. One of them is James Michener's *Texas* and the other, of course, McMurtry's *Lonesome Dove.* We have here, on the one hand, a famous outsider and an obviously nice man who spent several years directing his formidable energies to writing the saga of our state and, on the other, our most distinguished native-born author, the 1985 winner of the Texas Institute of Letters's special award for the work of a lifetime. Once again the question I asked as I read was: What do these books tell us about Texas women?

And the answer is: Not a great deal, because women play so small a part, relatively speaking, in those novels. Both books are very long, and, though I am not inclined to count

the pages, I don't think either devotes as much as ten percent
of its space to women. I calculate it closer to six. That fact itself is a powerful comment: two men as well-disposed as we
are likely to find do not feel obligated to give women equal
time. They don't see the essential Texas story as one in which
the women's role deserves equal attention. I don't mean to
suggest that we should apply affirmative action to literature,
but I do think we need to recognize a lopsided story when we
see one. They do not take as their primary subjects the relations
between men and women, as Thomas Hardy, for example,
does, or D. H. Lawrence and Henry James, if we want to keep
to the English literary tradition. This is partly a reflection of a
hard cultural truth about Texas that we would do well finally
to admit, and partly a failure of individual writers. But let's see
what we can learn from them when they do describe women.

Unlike McMurtry's, Michener's book takes on the whole
of Texas, past and present. He writes about several good
sturdy pioneer women, including Creoles and Mexican Americans, and he shows the mixing of Indian and Spanish in the
southern part of the state that produced some of the strongest
women among us. He writes a terrifying story of a young girl
captured by the Comanches whose ears and nose are burned
off but who survives and ultimately, as Faulkner might say,
even prevails.

Of course Michener also gives us some capable modern
women, and there are two who tell us something important
about Texas women and their relation to citizenship and political power: their relation therefore to self-government and
self-respect. The first is Miss Lorena Cobb, cotton heiress and
descendant of two United States senators:

> She was one of those standard Texas women, overawed
> in their twenties by the excessive machismo of their men,
> but emergent in their fifties as some of the most elegant
> and powerful females on earth. They formed the back-

bone of Texas cities, persuading their wealthy husbands and friends to build hospitals and museums, then dominating the society which resulted. Women like her made those of Massachusetts and New York seem downright anemic.

Several observations about Miss Cobb are in order, I think. One: she is white and extremely rich, so that very few other Texas women could aspire to exercising political power or influence in the way that she does. Two: by Michener's description, she has spent some three decades languishing under the "excessive machismo" of Texas men before she manages to come into her own; she does not exercise power until she is menopausal and therefore, perhaps, less threatening to men. Three: even her power is derivative; it depends on her ability to charm and to wheedle.

The second woman in Michener's book is a professor at TCU, and originally a Southerner. She is, I take it, a sociologist, and she speaks as follows:

> Texas today is Carolina of yesterday, and in no aspect of life is this more apparent than in your attitude toward women. You cherished us, honored us, protected us, but you also wanted us to stay to hell in our place. In no state of the Union does a woman enjoy a higher social status than in Texas. She is really revered. But in few states does she enjoy more limited freedoms. If I were, and God should be so generous, nineteen years old, with an eighteen-inch waist, flawless skin and flashing green eyes, I'd rather live in Texas than anywhere else, because I would be appreciated. But if I were the way I actually was at that age, thirty-one-inch waist, rather soggy complexion and an I.Q. hovering near a hundred and sixty, Texas would not be my chosen residence.

She goes on to point out that the things women are traditionally thought to favor—things associated with compassion, fairness, generosity of spirit—have not fared well politically: "In public education," she says, Texas has been "very tardy in establishing schools, very niggardly in paying for them. In public services, except roads, among the least generous in the nation. In health services, care for children, care for the aged, provisions for prisoners, always near the bottom." In James Michener's eyes, then, Texas women have been and are paid considerable sentimental and rhetorical attention. They have been forced, however, to limit their real influence to a very narrow circle.

As for McMurtry's *Lonesome Dove,* he is writing here solely about the past: about the frontier, a place an early immigrant said was "heaven for men and dogs; hell for women and oxen"—a place McMurtry himself had earlier explicitly described as masculine and appealing, he thought, "because it offers an acceptable orientation to violence." Therefore, when he writes what his publishers describe as "the long-awaited, epic masterpiece of the American West," we know that he has turned his back on his more recent fictional explorations of urban life, and therefore of women, and gone back to the world where men hold undisputed mastery. Whether or not we think of this reversion to his earlier subjects as a failure of nerve, we cannot expect women to play a major role in *Lonesome Dove,* and they do not.

But there are two very attractive women in his new book, and each of them, I think, has something valuable to reveal about our topic. One of them, Lorena Wood, is a beautiful young whore, as engaging and convincing as any I know in fiction. McMurtry is very clear about the economic and biographical facts that drove her to prostitution, and by making her so strong and appealing, it seems to me he implicitly criticizes the middle-class values to which most Texas women cling that dig an impassable gulf between the "good woman" and the whore.

The other is Clara, who loved the Ranger hero Gus Mc-
Crae but who married instead a phlegmatic, kindly man on
whom she thought she could better depend. Her decision puts
into ironic perspective the whole cowboy myth; it reveals how
alien all its virtues are to the necessary building blocks of
community—to the relations between men and women and to
the upbringing of children. At the end she rages at Woodrow
Call, who has been Gus's companion for half a century: "I'm
sorry you and Gus McCrae ever met. All you two done was
ruin one another, not to mention those close to you. . . . I
didn't want to fight you for him every day of my life. You men
and your promises: they're just excuses to do what you plan to
do anyway, which is leave. You think you've always done
right—that's your ugly pride, Mr. Call. But you never did
right and it would be a sad woman that needed anything
from you. You're a vain coward, for all your fighting. I de-
spised you then, for what you were, and I despise you now,
for what you're doing."

Now Clara is drawn as a splendid woman and Woodrow
Call as one of the heroes of *Lonesome Dove,* which makes this
outburst all the more startling: the most admirable woman in
the book is made to despise one of the most admirable men.
There's a glimmer here of something McMurtry does not
develop.

And it makes me wish that a woman would take the
figure of Clara and write a book from her angle of vision:
Rangers, cattle drives, and the frontier West as the tough-
minded, self-reliant Clara might see it. The kinds of things she
does are no more mundane than following cows' rumps hundreds of miles to Montana, yet the cowboy has been made into
a figure of romance and women like her have not.

I do not mean to suggest that we need any more roman-
ticizing about Texas. But most men simply cannot tell women's
stories: they tell reality skewed; they tell it wonky. I find little
hint, really, of the Texas women—black, brown, or white—

whom I know best in any of this writing. I cannot find my own context, my own roots in their books, much less do they hint where women like Minnie Fisher Cunningham, Jessie Daniel Ames, Dorothy Gebauer, Sissy Farenthold, Barbara Jordan, Anne Armstrong, or Ann Richards might come from. And if I, a white woman close to some of those male writers, find their work alien, I have no trouble imagining how remote it must seem to black women and Chicanas.

In talking about her work on *The Color Purple,* Alice Walker remembers that when a certain black male critic heard she might write a historical novel, he said, in effect, heaven forbid. She suspected that his response came from his knowing that her "history" would not begin "with the taking of lands, or the births, battles, and deaths of Great Men, but with one woman asking another for her underwear." Precisely. I don't think our stories will have anything like the same shape men's stories have, and certainly not the same values. "Winning" will not be the same, or "progress." Violence will not be glorified, and neither will the many social forms of contempt.

But I think it is important that we not be sentimental about our subjects. When we write about Texas women there are several fundamental facts about their lives that have narrowed the scope of their experience and worked to cripple their imagination. With apologies for my broad, crude strokes, I'd like to sketch them.

One of those facts is that until very recently, most women were denied a normal, healthy sexuality. Everything worked against it: the dangers of childbirth, the absence of effective contraception, ignorance, fear, propriety, even racism. On the basis of the evidence I have uncovered, it would seem only a slight exaggeration to say that in the early days of Texas, women tended to be either the hausfrau or the whore. On the one side were freedom, sexuality, and fun, or what passed for

them at that time and place. On the other, too many children
and work that was exhausting and confining. The double standard was apparently rigidly enforced; as the cowboy Teddy
Blue said, "If I'd have been a woman and done what I done,
I'd have ended up in a sporting house." "Good women" had
no dealings with the other kind, and community feeling against
"loose living" ran high. Jim Hogg wrote his daughter Ima, "a
woman's character is her capital," and I suspect that the req-
uisite sexual repression, along with the chasm between the
good woman—the pure woman—and the whore may be
largely responsible for weaving the great, thick pall of propriety that has hung over the lives of so many women. Experience muddies purity, and therefore good women must not
seek it. The women who came before us forced on themselves
the kind of denial that so often twists and cripples the spirit.
They taught themselves to confine their lives within a safe,
predictable circle.

Second: despite the popular images of fabulous wealth,
for a good deal of their history, most Texas women have also
been poor, and for whatever money they enjoyed, they typi-
cally had to depend on men—usually their husbands, sometimes their employers. One of the most powerful descriptions
of what that poverty meant in the lives of Texas women comes
in Robert Caro's biography of Lyndon Johnson. If you read
his dazzling chapter "The Sad Irons," you will know what life
was like for Hill Country women before rural electrification:
what it was like to can fruits and vegetables over wood stoves
in summer heat that soared way past one hundred degrees;
what it was like to carry the water for the weekly family wash
from the distant well; what it was like to wash it all, and rinse
it all, and starch it all, and iron it all with irons that had to be
kept hot by resting them over open fires. Hard, repetitive
work has been the lot of all but a small portion of the women
here. As the German settler Mathilda Wagner wrote, "People

who have never gone through it can't realize how these people who started the little Texas towns and made them grow had to starve and do."

Third: Texas women have lived in a violent society. One of the most terrifying pieces of writing I've ever read is Rachel Parker Plummer's artless description of her two years' captivity with the Comanches, particularly the murder of her six-week-old baby. And violence women did not suffer themselves they often witnessed. Over a period of almost fifty years, for instance—from 1882 to 1930—492 people were lynched in Texas, making our state by that measure the third most violent in the nation.

Though the research on the subject is not complete, I do not believe that women naturally incline to violence; they do not characteristically choose violent ways to deal with their differences—perhaps for no more noble reason than that they aren't very well equipped physically to win. It was a Texas woman, Jessie Daniel Ames, who headed the ultimately successful white women's campaign against lynching. But violence has been a part of Texas from the beginning, from the wars with Mexico and between the Indians and the Anglo settlers, to the Civil War and the conflict over secession within the state; from the legal violence of slavery to the illegal violence of the Ku Klux Klan; from the casual bar killing by Saturday-night specials to the numbing brutalities of football all over the state. Some of that violence is glorified in Texas, and though I would not claim that women take no pleasure in it, I do think it puts us at a disadvantage always. At its most innocuous it turns us into a cheerleader culture; at its most dangerous, it brutalizes and kills us. In such a society, most women can ultimately be overpowered or overruled. The prevalence of violence therefore makes us guarded, reactive, dependent. It forces us to live in a world over which we have meager control.

Fourth: Texas women have lived in a racist society. Racism has exaggerated the tendency people have to stick with their own kind, so that most women here have not been able to enjoy in their own lives the amazing diversity of people who have settled in this state. Though the burdens of racism have obviously worked most severely against black and brown women, they have crippled whites as well. One of the legacies of slavery, for instance, has been the sexual suspicion between white women and black. The latter had lived for generations at the mercy of white men, and so we came out of that sordid period in our history with, on the one side, the white lady on the pedestal and, on the other, the myth of the black whore—a dichotomy that has not wholly lost its unhappy power to keep black and white women from knowing one another and coming together as friends and allies.

When I was growing up, I was not allowed to see black or brown girls as equals, and neither were any of my friends. We were taught that we were "better," and some of us have not yet had the chance to understand otherwise. When I was a senior at the University of Texas, a black woman was cast to sing Dido in Purcell's *Dido and Aeneas,* but the Board of Regents forced her out of the performance. Four years ago she made her debut at the Metropolitan Opera. I am sure Barbara Smith Conrad could not care less about knowing me, but I am convinced my life has been poorer for not knowing her.

Finally, the doctrine that woman's place is in the home held extraordinarily coercive power in limiting the degree to which women had influence over their own lives. Like their sisters elsewhere, Texas women had nothing directly to say about public policy until 1920, and it is much harder to change institutions that already exist than to shape them from the beginning. Nor have they yet achieved a voice as strong as their numbers warrant. Partly because of that hard political fact, almost 1,300,000 women here, or more than one in six, live even today in poverty. More than a million Texas children live in poverty, or almost one in four. Texas ranks forty-seventh among the states in the maximum aid it gives to dependent children, and less than one-third of our poor children are covered by the Women and Infant Children program.

Our typical Texas woman, then, has been sexually deprived and poor, dependent on men for the money that bought her bread. She has been vulnerable to violence, crippled by racism, and muffled politically. In order to build stable lives and communities, as we saw in Clara's tirade aginst Woodrow Call in *Lonesome Dove,* she has had to counter the male instinct to wander the plains or, as Huck Finn put it, "to light out for the Territory." She has had to fight the patronizing of even good men like John Graves, who sneers at "sober, useful, decent people [who] build for themselves sober, useful, decent lives." And of course there have been other primary antagonists in our story. The wind, as Dorothy Scarborough told us. The tornadoes and the hurricanes. The sand. The immense, flat land. And the heat.

But despite all her terrible disadvantages, that typical Texas woman brought up children and kept families together. She raised and cooked their food; made and maintained their clothes; worked to make their shelters life-enhancing. She planted fruits and flowers and created much of what grace there has been in daily life. She moved from the farms and prairies to hamlets and then to towns and to cities, weaving the fabric of community as she went. She taught in schools and tended the sick. She filled the churches, which have been the major institutional force in this state that has worked to make a gentler ethic prevail. She helped others live and helped them die.

She deserves our attention on her merits, and for our own sakes we need to pay it. We need to know so much more than we do about how she tried to do those things: what barriers she faced, what help she found in charting the ways over or around them, what she felt like while she persevered and what she turned to when she failed.

And so I profoundly distrust our mythology, along with much of the male writing on our state, and I come away from my immersion in our most prominent fiction convinced that women need to write about Texas, past and present. Furthermore, all of us need to learn our history and share it with one another, so that we can understand more fully than most of us do today what it means to be a Texas woman. As Carol Christ has written: "Without stories a woman is lost when she comes to make the important decisions of her life. She does not learn to value her struggles, to celebrate her strengths, to comprehend her pain. Without stories she cannot understand herself. Without stories she is alienated from those deeper experiences of self and world that have been called spiritual or religious. She is closed in silence."

For those of us who want to know where women fit into the Texas scheme of things, there is a strong nucleus already, beginning for me with Dorothy Scarborough's astonishing novel *The Wind*—a high plains *Tess of the d'Urbervilles* and *Wuthering Heights* combined. The most widely read and interesting women novelists writing from or about Texas today include Shelby Hearon, Beverly Lowry, and Laura Furman. We have Ruthe Winegarten's valuable bibliography and her *Texas Women: A Pictorial History*. We are blessed with such finely documented and important studies as Jacquelyn Dowd Hall's *Revolt against Chivalry* and Sandra L. Myres's *Westering Women*, as well as Jo Ella Exley's edition of women's letters and reminiscences, *Texas Tears and Texas Sunshine*. But I did not come across those works as a matter of course, and neither have any of my Texas friends. We have been much less aware of women's work than of the writing of certain men. Not only do we need very much more of the former; we need to make sure it becomes a part of the ordinary Texan's consciousness.

Some of the best journalists writing here today are

women: Kaye Northcott, Molly Ivins, and Barbara Karkabi
spring first to my mind. The present, therefore, is less prob-
lematic for our purposes than the past. And since we can never
know all we want to know about the women who helped build
Texas because most of them were too busy working to keep
records, to some extent we must imagine, depending therefore
on fiction for its larger understandings.

Even Katherine Anne Porter, who grew up here, has
been neglected by the official cultural apparatus of our state.
McMurtry notes that she suffered from being "genteel to the
core," and finds that her best work demonstrates the triumph
of the artist in her over the lady, a perception that underscores,
however obliquely, the basic argument I am making here.
Nevertheless, she deserves far more attention than she has
gotten in Texas.

Furthermore, women writers outside our tradition can
also help us feel what life inside may have been. We can look,
for instance, to Alice Walker's *The Color Purple,* Lee Smith's
Oral History, and Carolyn Chute's *The Beans of Egypt, Maine*
for what it tastes and smells and feels like to be poor. We can
read Joan Chase's *During the Reign of the Queen of Persia* for a
sense of life in rural isolation. We can trust to Paule Marshall
or Toni Morrison for our understanding of the price blacks
often pay for their struggle to enter the middle class and main-
stream America. We can read Walker's *Meridian* and Rosellen
Brown's *Civil Wars* to sense more deeply the human struggle
embedded in the civil rights movement, one of the two great
struggles for justice in our lifetime, and to Bobbie Ann Ma-
son's *In Country* for a finer understanding of what happened to
us because of Vietnam. We can immerse ourselves in Anne
Tyler for her celebration of ordinary people. And for an almost Tolstoyan view of a culture from the eyes of a woman—
for a drama of generations of women and men in often deadly
combat—we can look to Latin America and Isabel Allende's

intensely sexual, intensely political *The House of the Spirits.* Jonathan Yardley, dean of book reviewing on the *Washington Post,* has decreed, rather petulantly, that women are writing the best fiction today, and we need to draw gratefully on that.

The great popularity of the Women in Texas exhibit that traveled several years ago and lodges now at Texas Woman's University in Denton showed how starved so many of us are for the nourishing food of our past. In the spring of 1986, Southwestern University in Georgetown devoted its annual Brown Symposium to the theme "Womanhood, Manhood and Public Life: Visions and Revisions of Gender in America," and a few weeks later the University of Texas sponsored the first formal gathering of Texas women scholars. The movement to recover Texas women and finally take them seriously is well underway.

Ladies in the old-fashioned sense cannot leave their pedestals, nor can they ask hard questions in search of disconcerting answers. I hope, therefore, that we can leave propriety and dependence behind in the interests of a richer life and a more searing truth. We will not find answers to all our questions, but we can find many if we seek in the spirit of the seventeenth-century French midwife, Louise Bourgeois, who said, "Undertake, till the last day of your life, to learn, which to do readily requires a great humbleness, for the proud do not win the hearts of those who know secrets."

PALEFACES VS. REDSKINS: A LITERARY SKIRMISH

Don Graham

> It is quite all right to regard me as a Southern, specifi-
> cally a Texas, writer.
> —Katherine Anne Porter to George Sessions Perry,
>   February 1943

The Texas literary scene today reminds me of the skirmish
line a famous critic once saw in the landscape of American
literature. Philip Rahv said it was the Palefaces versus the
Redskins, Henry James vs. Mark Twain. On one side, culture,
refinement, and technique; on the other, raw life, realism, and
maybe something less than art. In Texas terms, Katherine
Anne Porter vs. J. Frank Dobie. Such polarities are of course
complex when you get down to actual cases. In a work like
Noon Wine Porter wrote about the Redskin side with consum-
mate power; and Dobie, who devoted a lifetime to studying
the Redskin past—Old Texas, the ranching tradition, cowboys—lusted after Paleface status.

Today the Paleface-Redskin issue is in full swing, and the
sides are clearly lined up. The Palefaces are all those folks
who stand ready to rescue Texas writing (and indeed Texas
itself) from its provincial, embarrassing, and nativistic roots.
Many of the Palefaces are emigrés, recent arrivals, but many
are homegrown, too. All are the literary equivalent to Yup-

This essay first appeared in the November-December 1984 issue of the
Texas Humanist, published by the Texas Committee for the Humanities.

pies: upscale, well-educated, fern-bar writers. The Paleface world view is pretty simple, and it looks like this:

EAST	*TEXAS*
Ideas	*Prejudices*
Sensitivity	*Chauvinism*
Art	*Ort*

Palefaces tend to cluster in the major cities and many earn their bread in the academies teaching creative writing. Houston is probably the capital of Paleface Writing Culture, as any Houston-based writer will be happy to tell you. Houston has managed to lure back to Texas the best of the Paleface writers, Donald Barthelme. Now Barthelme is a very fine writer indeed, and any state ought to be glad to claim him. But with two or three tiny exceptions, none of Barthelme's work takes the measure of Texas—or tries to—though it does do an excellent job of capturing the *frissons* of upper Manhattan. Redskins tend to live out where the screwworms kill the cows. Elmer Kelton, for example, lives in San Angelo; Jane Gilmore Rushing in Lubbock; and Pat Ellis Taylor, late of Austin, now resides in a rundown suburb of El Paso.

Maybe where you drink is a better index than where you live. In Austin the ultimate Paleface-Yuppie drinking hole is a eucalyptus bar overlooking Lake Travis, with a multi-tiered, many-splendored view of the lake, the circling buzzards, and the falling waterline in this time of drought. Here, every sunset, the pilgrims from New Jersey and California come to sip their Perriers and strawberry daiquiris and genteelly applaud the sinking of the sun in the west. With every high-rise, every art deco bar, Redskin Texas fades a little more into the sunset. It's a good subject, this time of change and loss and gain, and our best writers, Redskin and Paleface, will have things to tell us about the way we live now.

But for now, the culture battle rages on. Who's winning?

The Palefaces. In the end they nearly always win. They've already taken over the Texas Institute of Letters. Two out of the last three years, the top prize ($5,000 cold American) has gone to books that have absolutely nothing to do with Texas: the 1981 winner dealt with bachelor life in New York City, the 1983 winner with the international tennis circuit. Mr. Bachelor had barely touched down at the Houston airport before the Prize was his, and Mr. Tennis, who taught in Austin for a while, has lived in Rome the last three years. TIL membership has tilted, too. Of late, the fern-bar, emigré, or expatriate literary mag crowd has been admitted by the gross, while outsiders, native Texans writing in and of the state, languish at Dairy Queens and honky-tonks, exiles in their native land. Brie anyone?

The Palefaces are bothered most by Texas "vulgarity" and "anti-intellectualism." I embrace the first. Wanna see my surgical scars? Wanna have a conference in the toilet? Lyndon, thou should'st be living at this hour; Texas hath need of thee. Anti-intellectualism is a meaner charge, and as someone who has spent a lifetime among books, ideas, and ort, I resent being accused, as I was recently, of anti-intellectualism. The case against me? I had pooh-poohed French cinema critics for their overestimation of certain American films. For this I am called anti-intellectual. Where's my shooting iron?

From similar fears, I think, most writers don't like being labeled as Texas writers or even regionalists for that matter. They just want to be called Writers. Fine. But still, I think, there's something to be said for looking at writers within the context of a culture, a place. That's what I do for a living, in part: I teach a course at the University of Texas called Life and Literature of the Southwest. When J. Frank Dobie first proposed such a course, back in 1929, the story goes that the English Department declared there wasn't any Southwestern literature. (American literature as a separate field of study was only beginning to achieve independent status during this same era.) So Dobie said, All right, there's plenty of life; I'll teach that.

Today, in the post-Dobie era, there's plenty of literature. But is there a Texas literary tradition? I think there is, but it exists apart from the knowledge of the writers themselves. Writers have other fish to fry, they read eclectically, and they often haven't read the work of their predecessors and peers, for dozens of good and sufficient reasons. If you look at the responses of Texas writers collected in Patrick Bennett's *Talking with Texas Writers,* it becomes overwhelmingly obvious that most of the writers Bennett interviewed have not read very widely in the imaginative literature produced by earlier Texas writers. There is no mention of such writers as Edwin Lanham, Mary King, William Barney, John W. Wilson, and many others I could name who have produced Texas works of value and artistic merit.

Where does this situation leave us? With plenty to do. The task for academics is to do what they do best, to uncover, sift through, evaluate, and redeem from the past that which is valuable and worth knowing. The task for Texas writers is to stop worrying about *Texas* as a provincial tag, a handicap, a brand. The task for publishers is to take chances, print original new Texas fiction, and reprint the classics. Newspapers and magazines need to review Texas books, and here the record is extremely spotty. Too many Texas newspapers carry no book reviews at all, or devote all their space to swooning over the latest fiction published by Norman Mailer or Joyce Carol Oates while allowing good Texas fiction to sink into obscurity. Finally, the public needs to buy Texas fiction, add new titles to personal Southwestern libraries, and stop depending on the best-seller lists to tell them what to read.

With increased knowledge instead of fifth-rate opinions based on cultural differences, brie vs. barbecue, maybe then the Paleface-Redskin controversy can level off, TIL can start operating the way it should (or else drop Texas from the name of the organization), and everybody can recognize that Texas, a big country, has room for every kind of writer under the sun.

Postscript, 1987

When my remarks on the Texas literary scene appeared in 1984, I received several postcards from writers scattered hither and yon—one, I recall, came all the way from London, England—and all said they considered themselves in the Redskin camp. Then silence, the usual response, set in, and I went about my business, going for whole weeks without ever thinking about Texas literary skirmishes.

Imagine my surprise, then, when Donald Barthelme, two years later, in 1986, took out after me in *Texas Monthly*. My portrait of the new Texas writers provoked him to inquire, "Did he mean faggot homosexual queer pansy fairies? And if so, why didn't he say so?" Very odd, this sexual reading of my argument. It seemed obvious to me that all I had meant by "fern-bar writer" was the kind of writer who lacked any close or meaningful relation with a specific place. Deracination was the point of my argument. It had nothing to do with the sexual inclinations of anybody.

It's probably time to drop the armed-camp metaphor. Most native Texans have their feet in two worlds: Redskin past, Paleface present. I don't want to turn the clock back, return to live on a starve-out farm or in a small town where there are no libraries, no theaters, no museums, no restaurants. Nor, in reading, do I want to have to choose between George Sessions Perry's Rockdale or Bud Shrake's Dallas. Country, town, city—Texas regionalism can encompass them all.

ARBITERS OF TEXAS LITERARY TASTE

James Ward Lee

For many years—from the mid-twenties to the late fifties—
J. Frank Dobie acted as the self-appointed literary dictator of
Texas. Until near the end of his life in 1964, J. Frank Dobie
was "the man to see" about Texas literary and folkloristic
matters, and he decided which other people were to be seen
about history, politics, and education in Texas. If a New York
magazine editor wanted to do a spread on Texas, he picked up
the phone and called Dobie in Austin. If a book publisher
needed a preface written for a book about the Southwest, he
asked Dobie to write it or to suggest a substitute. No pro-
nouncement about Texas had sanction unless J. Frank Dobie
uttered it—or at least authorized its utterance.

Much to the surprise of some, Dobie was mortal, and
when he died, his mantle fell on the shoulders of SMU professor Lon Tinkle, author of *13 Days to Glory* (the book was
filmed as *The Alamo*) and, fittingly, a biography of J. Frank
Dobie. So from the mid-fifties to the late seventies, Tinkle was

---

"Arbiters of Texas Literary Taste" was delivered as a speech on several
occasions during 1984 and 1985.

the arbiter of literary taste in Texas—a role he had prepared for by long service as the main spokesman for the best that had been thought and said in Dallas. When Tinkle died in 1978, the Dobie throne fell vacant once again. And at the moment a power struggle seems to be shaping up between Dallas journalist and all-purpose man of letters A. C. Greene and former Texan Larry McMurtry, who occasionally fires off a blast at Texas, Texans, and Southwest writing from his rare-book store in Georgetown, in the District of Columbia.

I suspect that both McMurtry and Greene would deny having designs on the unofficial post as Imperial Potentate of Texas Literary Matters. But I am equally sure that neither would be loath to sit on the throne long occupied by James Frank Dobie—who styled himself "Pancho." Why would either want the unpaid post? Because everyone loves to be consulted, especially by "the networks." The thrill of having CBS or the *Times* call and ask for an opinion, or at least a quote, must never wear off. Even Pulitzer Prize–winner McMurtry must get a thrill when he hears that Bill Moyers or Jim Lehrer or Dan Rather (each of whom is himself a Texas arbiter of some note) is on the phone. And then the very idea of being the leader of a coterie, as Dobie certainly was, probably appeals to almost everyone. Picture it: aspiring writers fall as silent as E. F. Hutton's listeners when you speak; people holding literary conferences stake everything on getting you to appear; admirers drive halfway across Texas in blinding rainstorms to hear you read aloud; universities pay enough to feed a battalion of assistant professors in order to have you spend time "in residence"; and, who knows, Cambridge may call you—it did Dobie. But the main satisfaction may come in having people hang on your every word. And your words don't really have to make such sense. Witness what Dobie wrote in a preface to Andy Adams's *The Log of a Cowboy:* "[It] is the best book that has ever been written about cowboy life, and it is the best book that ever can be written about cowboy life." The absolute absurdity of that statement has not kept it from being quoted again and again by disciples of Dobie— many of whom should have known better. I saw it quoted most recently by Don Graham, who is only a couple of places behind Greene and McMurtry in the line of succession to the Dobie throne. Unlike many who had quoted it before, Graham knew its absurdity and was using it in an article that proved— to me at least—that Benjamin Capps's *The Trail to Ogallala* is far superior to *Log*, "the best book that ever can be written about cowboy life." As a matter of fact, there are a dozen better treatments of cowboy life than Adams's. Dobie's comment on Adams, written for one of his myriad prefaces, had the authority of scripture to his followers. And what is worse, it still does. It takes courage even today for a commentator on Texas writing to challenge one of Dobie's ex cathedra manifestos.

The most interesting fact about Dobie's career as the Great Cham of Texas literature is his almost total ignorance of literary matters. He became a literary dictator without taste and without serious study. He knew nothing about literature, but he knew what he liked. He liked books about cowboys, Indians, Texas Rangers, mustangs, humble Mexicans, ranch life, and buried treasure. He liked for Texas, which was a Deep South state for most of his life, to be pictured as the Far West, the Wild West. He wanted America to forget that in Texas cotton was king, that the state had joined the Rebellion, and that the outlook of the majority of its citizens had been Confederate. In short, he wanted to rewrite history. The maddening thing is that he pulled it off. He made almost everyone forget that most Texans lived east of the Brazos, that cotton and timber rescued the state from the post–Civil War depression, and that there were more farmers than cowboys in the Lone Star State.

Dobie's career was the result of his cleverness as a self-promoter, his untiring ambition, some facility as a journalist, and the fact that Texas can always use an "interpreter" to the nation: Texas is phenomenal, and someone has to explain the phenomena. Widely admired as a folklorist, Dobie was, in actuality, little more than an adapter of folktales. Many of his contemporaries thought him a stylist, but his writing is stilted and awkward. He saw himself as a philosopher, but there is little evidence that he ever got past the clichés of philosophy. (Over Dobie's fireplace at Paisano Ranch west of Austin is carved "Fire is the greatest philosopher"; that, I think, may say it all about the great man's philosophical pretensions.) His legions of admirers hailed him as a great raconteur, and it was perhaps as an oral storyteller that he achieved his greatest success. His yarn-spinning in classes in Texana at the University of Texas is legendary. I still wonder how good he really was, though, for when I saw him telling stories to the Texas Folklore Society toward the end of his life—about 1959—I did not find him impressive. His old students and some of his fellow folklorists still saw the magic, but I wonder if they did not half create a glory that I was not able to see. I merely saw an old man dressed like Mark Twain, perhaps even seeing himself as a Brush Country Innocent Abroad. But there was little real resemblance to the famous Missourian.

There is no doubt that the man was a genius as a promoter. If he had turned his hand to commerce, he might have driven half the state's millionaires into bankruptcy. From his various platforms—a Sunday newspaper column, a radio station in San Antonio, a lecture hall at the University of Texas, a post as secretary-editor of the Texas Folklore Society, a charter membership in the Texas Institute of Letters, positions on Texas Centennial committees—from all these posts he lectured Texans on their heritage and on the literature that he saw fit to approve. His posturing as the grand old sage began before he was forty. But that pose, like all his others, was pure magic—and this is in a state that has no shortage of poseurs, a state that made heroes of LBJ and H. L. Hunt and Howard Hughes and Racehorse Haynes and Glenn McCarthy, to name a few pretty fair hands at posing and self-promoting. I am not sure anyone on the list above could top J. Frank Dobie when it came to self-advertisement. He was helped in his aggrandizement by Walter Prescott Webb, a noted historian, and Roy Bedichek, a man who took up writing when he was near seventy and who became a member of the "Holy Trinity of Texas Letters" on the basis of one book: *Adventures with a Texas Naturalist.* (Bedichek also wrote a book on the sense of smell and a history of the Texas Interscholastic League, but *Adventures* is the volume that made it possible for Dobie to canonize him.) Dobie, Bedichek, and Webb became the revered triumvirate and are still seen as such by hundreds and hundreds of Texans. In many places it is still blasphemy to utter a sentence critical of these grand old men, and it is to Larry McMurtry's credit that he has tried in at least two essays to show just how inflated their reputations were.

Despite all the anecdotes about Dobie, Bedichek, and Webb, despite all the reverence displayed by their followers, and even despite some writings by them that I admire, I am unable to see what all the fuss was about. Webb was a competent—sometimes brilliant—historian who wrote boring books. Bedichek was a curiosity, an old schoolman who started a new career in his seventh decade. But Dobie was a mesmerist who was able to attract to his cause many who were more talented and intelligent than he was. It is still puzzling to me how he managed to turn himself into *the* arbiter of literary taste in Texas. The closest thing we have to a present-day Dobie is a certain kind of popular newspaper columnist, usually a manly sort of sentimentalist, who writes feelingly about old dogs and children and attacks the degradations and deprivations of modern life. These writers often develop such a following among the culturally desperate that they are taken seriously no matter how far out of their depth they get.

As noted earlier, Dobie's stay on this earth was limited. When he went to join the immortals, he left things Texan in the capable hands of Lon Tinkle of Dallas. Tinkle had been a major figure in the Texas Institute of Letters for years before Dobie's death; in fact, Tinkle had become *the* moving force behind the Institute in the late forties. I suspect that Dobie was playing at being a sage by then and was glad to have Tinkle do the work of the TIL. Tinkle did a good job with an organization that was often laughed at as an attempt to be a French Academy of the prairies. Even though the organization may sometimes be a bit pretentious, it performs a number of useful functions. The Institute awards prizes for writing by Texans or quasi-Texans or outsiders passing as Texans (the rules are too complicated to explain; it is harder to get into the Kingdom of Heaven, but it is simpler). The Institute also makes literary pronouncements upon occasion. For instance, when Larry McMurtry writes a particularly anti-Texan piece, the press calls the president, the secretary, or the most prominent member (or all of the above) for a statement. And on one or two occasions, the Institute has spoken effectively against Texas's brand of censorship. The TIL is a pretty good platform for a person who has pretensions to literary dictatorship, and Lon Tinkle did.

His reign was benevolent, and in almost all ways good for Texas writers and Texas writing. Tinkle, a professor of French at Southern Methodist University, was intelligent and educated, and he had a genuine love of literature—all kinds of literature. In most ways Lon Tinkle was the ideal spokesman for Texas letters: he had been book editor of the *Dallas Morning News*; he was a great organizer of SMU book-and-author luncheons that brought Eastern Establishment writers to Dallas; he traveled extensively on the ladies literary circuit in

Dallas; and he had always used his contacts with the rich to award more and larger prizes to Texas writers. And, most important, he was a voice ever ready to speak for learning and for literature in a Dallas still culturally raw—even by Texas standards. Tinkle was a thoroughly likable and nice man who seemed eager to help everyone he met—and he remembered everyone's name. It did not hurt at all that he actually looked like Mark Twain. He certainly had it on Dobie there.

Tinkle's death left a void that has not yet been completely filled. The Texas Institute of Letters fell into the hands of the *Texas Monthly* crowd for a time, and the organization became less interested in serious writing than in slick journalism. After the journalists had had their day with TIL, the organization was dominated by writers connected with two of the state's leading creative writing programs—one at SMU and the other at the University of Houston. (Don Graham calls this era the reign of the "Palefaces," but more about that later.) The Institute continues to reflect the strong influence of creative writing departments, though there are indications that it is becoming more eclectic. Some critics of TIL have argued that it became a feminist organization in the late seventies and on into the eighties. It is true that Shelby Hearon, Beverly Lowry, and Kaye Northcott were all elected to terms as president and a number of the Paisano Fellows have been women in recent years, but I see no indication that the organization has changed its orientation from writing to politics, sexual or otherwise. In any case, powerful as the TIL is in the Texas literary world, neither its president nor its secretary is automatically heir apparent to the Dobie throne.

In the last few years, A. C. Greene, often called the Dean of Texas Letters (when John Graves is not being called the Dean), has begun to emerge as a serious force in the Institute and as the main spokesman for literary Texas to the world at large. Greene is an ideal replacement for Tinkle. He is ubiquitous. If a literary luncheon or a panel discussion about writing or a newspaper interview on Texas letters or a literary conference takes place, A. C. is likely to be present. Not only is he intelligent and well educated, but his training as a newspaper editor gives him the ability to speak in headlines, and journalists can count on him to provide them with quotable one-liners. In addition, Greene is willing to take on the chore of producing the Institute's occasional newsletters and doing other work that furthers the cause of writing in Texas. His *The Fifty Best Books on Texas* has become a Bible for booksellers and collectors of Texana—and it has driven the cost of many out-of-print books out of sight. Since 1986, he has been a member of the faculty of North Texas State University,* and his position as Coordinating Director of the Center for Texas Studies there has given him a forum that is almost as good as the one that Dobie had in Austin in the 1930s. Greene not only has a newspaper column in the *Dallas Morning News* and in syndication, he also has a signed column in *Texas Books in Review,* a quarterly book review journal that the Center for Texas Studies is now publishing. These outlets, plus his regular appearances on the "MacNeil/Lehrer Newshour" on national public television, make A. C. the definite heir apparent to the Dobie throne—if not already its occupant. Greene uses the media well. He praises Texas writers and generally tries to promote the cause of Texas literature when he can.

Nevertheless, Larry McMurtry still broods "like an aged eagle" over the literary scene in the Lone Star State. Everytime Greene seems to have his position solidified as "the man to call" in Texas, Larry McMurtry bursts violently onto the scene, either with a new book that dazzles the public or with one of his famous diatribes against Texas letters.

---

*In May 1988 North Texas State University officially became the University of North Texas. The older name has been retained in all essays written prior to that change.

For some years now, Larry McMurtry has, from time to time, felt the urge to befoul the nest that fledged him. When he is having one of his fits, he usually sets out to destroy the Holy Trinity of Dobie, Bedichek, and Webb before moving on to attack on an even broader front. The fact that he is right about the quality of the famed triumvirate does not automatically make him right about everything else. His first attack on the Texas Establishment goes back to 1961 or '62. Dobie noted in his copy of McMurtry's *Leaving Cheyenne* that its author had won the Texas Institute of Letters Award for his first novel— *Horseman, Pass By*—and had made a speech "giving the Texas Institute of Letters hell. I did not get details of his dissatisfaction." (Incidentally, Dobie was sent a copy of *Horseman, Pass By* in galley proofs and noted on the proofs, "If 'ripeness' were all, Larry McMurtry wouldn't get much of a grade." He did not review the book. And he refused even to read *Leaving Cheyenne.* It is barely possible that Dobie's dismissal of McMurtry did not set well. It is an undisputed fact that something about Dobie did not set well with McMurtry.) In 1968 McMurtry wrote an essay entitled "Southwestern Literature?" With emphasis on the question mark, he said. The essay blasted Dobie, et al., and generally raked Texas writers over the coals. It predicted great things for some of McMurtry's literary friends—Grover Lewis, Dave Hickey, William Harrison, and June Arnold among others. The callow essay didn't cause much of a stink except among his devoted followers. They loved the attack upon Dobie-Webb-Bedichek.

McMurtry's 1981 salvo is a different matter. Published in the *Texas Observer,* the essay grew out of a speech that the writer had given in Fort Worth. Entitled "Ever a Bridegroom: Reflections on the Failure of Texas Literature," the essay vilifies the ghosts of DobWebChek, berates their fellow travelers, damns a couple of authors with faint praise, dismisses some of the state's better writers, fails to acknowledge the existence of a number of Texas's best novelists, and attempts to promote—

once again—the works of some of his friends. And those are merely openers. What McMurtry is really suggesting—or demanding—is that other writers do as he has done: give up writing about farm and ranch and start dealing with what he calls the "less simplistic experience of city life." And another thing: Texas writers need to read the classics as McMurtry has done and not confine themselves to reading the works of other Texas writers. The insular nature of most Texas writers, he seems to think, grows from their limited reading programs. One gets a picture of McMurtry sitting in the Virginia Hunt Country thumbing his well-worn copy of *The Brothers Karamazov* preparatory to writing such recent masterpieces as *Cadillac Jack* and *The Desert Rose.*

One can't be sure what McMurtry's purpose was in his essay, but I suspect that he was promoting his urban novels. He has disavowed his earlier, rural novels—his best work, as most of his critics know—and is in a snit because readers don't understand how good *Terms of Endearment* really is. Now that *Lonesome Dove* has won a Pulitzer Prize and *Texasville* has garnered a wide readership, McMurtry may retire from the pamphlet wars and accept the laurels he deserves and that were, at long last, recently awarded by the *New York Review of Books,* which even included a David Levine cartoon alongside its review. (McMurtry is probably the only graduate of Archer City High School who has been caricatured by Levine.)

It is interesting to note that both *Lonesome Dove* and *Texasville* are set outside the cities; both are what McMurtry had derided in 1981 as "pastoral." I should be more generous. Everyone has a right to change his mind. But I am not sure that McMurtry has changed his mind. It is quite possible that he views *Lonesome Dove* and *Texasville* as "entertainments," the way Graham Greene does his thrillers. I am not prepared to bet that McMurtry won't later on reject his newest "pastorals" in one of his decadal diatribes on Texas writers and writings. It would not be uncharacteristic.

I have never been sure what to make of McMurtry's periodic outbursts. I am not at all sure that he wants to be "Mr. Texas." But neither am I certain that he doesn't. At first glance, it would seem that such a nasty piece of work as "Ever a Bridegroom" would do little to establish him as the Dobie of the eighties. But think again. Attacks on Texas always play well in New York—and in Dallas, Austin, Houston, Denton, and maybe, for heaven's sake, in Dalhart and Dumas. Some Texans are embarrassed at being Texans—that is what John Connally said was wrong with LBJ. Maybe McMurtry's attack had method. Maybe he meant to endear himself to those Texans who are fond of apologizing for not having been born in some more "cultured" state. I witnessed a masochistic thrill run through an audience that McMurtry addressed about eighteen months after his 1981 anti-Texas article appeared. In the spring of 1983, McMurtry joined a panel discussion at the University of Texas in honor of the university's centennial. Admirers and curiosity seekers came from miles around to see what he would say in the wake of his latest dash of vitriol. Beverly Lowry said from the stage that many had probably come to see "Larry and A. C. duke it out." (A. C. and many other writers had answered McMurtry in the press following publication of "Ever a Bridegroom." One writer, Dan Jenkins, called McMurtry a boring writer of "boring books"—but that was before "the Prize.") I was in the audience that day, and I got the impression that several of the panelists couldn't wait for McMurtry to kick them again. Even fellow panelist A. C. Greene, never one to take attacks on Texas and Texans lightly and certainly not a man to relish the outlander's derision, reached over and patted McMurtry on the back and said, in avuncular fashion, "I think Larry here has done more for Texas literature than anybody since J. Frank Dobie." McMurtry looked about with his customary aloofness and said nothing.

The exchange in Austin does not signal that McMurtry

has beaten A. C. out for the Dobie throne—or even that he
would take it now that he has "the Prize." (I am sorry for
these intrusive asides, but here comes another. *Lonesome Dove*
won not only the Pulitzer Prize, but the Spur Award of the
Western Writers of America and the fiction award of the Texas
Institute of Letters. There is no question that *Lonesome Dove* is
a good novel—flawed but nevertheless good—but it should
be remembered that the Pulitzer Prize has long been laughed
at in highbrow circles. That is not to say that most of us would
reject it—as Sinclair Lewis did—but serious writers, as
McMurtry certainly is most of the time, have not thought well
of the journalistic accolade.)

At the present moment, A. C. is, as boxing writers say,
"ahead on points." Someone is going to have to knock him
out to take the title. It is always a mistake to predict how
things will finally turn out; therefore, I can't wait to make a
prediction. A. C. is going to be "the Great Cham" of Texas
letters for a few more years. When A. C. either relinquishes or
retires the cup, Don Graham will be the man to call. Graham
was interviewed on national television when the Republican
Convention was in Texas in 1984 (of course, A. C. was on all
four networks). When the multi-part Sesquicentennial program *Lone Star* was broadcast on PBS in Texas, it looked like
the Don and A. C. show. (I almost said the Graham-Greene
show, but I feared that someone would confuse those two stal-
warts with the Catholic novelist whom Kingsley Amis calls
Grim Grin.) Don't forget, Don already occupies the Dobie
chair, so to speak. When Graham is quoted in the newspapers,
the reader is always told that Don Graham teaches the course
at the University of Texas that J. Frank Dobie invented. I don't
know whether Graham makes it a point to mention that or
whether it is one of those journalistic tag lines like "badly de-
composed body" or "hitherto unimpeachable source."

Like McMurtry and Greene, Graham is a fast man with a

quotable line. His essay on the creative writing schools several years ago has become notorious. He divided the state's writers into "Redskins" and "Palefaces," the Palefaces being those non-Texans who had been imported as creative writers to teach at such places as the University of Houston, the University of Texas, and SMU. He labeled some of the imports—and a few natives—"fern-bar writers" and treated them with some of the same contempt that hostile critics used to lavish on Salinger and what they called "the *New Yorker* school." The attack drew blood. Not long after its publication, Graham was inducted into the Texas Institute of Letters. At the TIL's annual gathering that year, he was introduced to one Houston writer, Phillip Lopate, by an Iago-like well-wisher. After a strained greeting, Lopate is reported to have exited abruptly, mentioning with irony that he had to go look for the closest fern bar. Stories like that help make Dobie heirs apparent.*

If Graham falters, Tom Pilkington is always a heartbeat away from Texas literary dictatorship. Pilkington is former editor of *Texas Books in Review,* coeditor of the present volume, coproducer/director of a videotape entitled *Texas Literature: The Southern Experience,* founding editor of TCU Press's *The Texas Tradition Series* and present coeditor of a similar series at SMU Press, coeditor of *The Texas Literary Tradition,* a senior editor of *A Literary History of the American West,* former president of the Western Literature Association, and author of many articles and books on Texas and Southwestern writing. Pilkington is not as fast with a quip as either Graham or Greene, but he is one of the finest scholars of Texas and Western literature in the country. He is one of the unquestioned leaders in Texas studies and a name "to conjure with," as they

---

*Since I wrote these paragraphs, I have learned that Don Graham has been named J. Frank Dobie Regents Professor of English and American Literature at the University of Texas. I rest my case.

say in political movies. (I have never understood that phrase
exactly, but I love it and am happy to be able, finally, to find a
use for it.)

And then some misguided critics have even gone so far as
to suggest that a darkhorse candidate is the present director of
the Center for Texas Studies at North Texas State University
and the author of *Classics of Texas Fiction*. Modesty forbids my
mentioning his name—and anyway, not only is he fond of the
discursive aside (in parentheses, of course), but he is from
Leeds, Alabama, not good credentials for one striving to be an
Arbiter of Literary Taste in Texas.

THE REPUBLIC OF TEXAS LETTERS

Marshall Terry

Coming from Ohio as a romantic, westering boy thirty-five years ago, I found Texas to be a warm, vital, distinctive state with plenty of the old frontier values and quirks still alive in it in the cities as well as the country. I meant to go on west, but I loved Texas for its vitality and diversity from the first moment I crossed its border, and so I stayed. My lifework has been for the most part teaching and the definition and implementation of an educational philosophy and curriculum in one of the few private universities on this recent frontier, but along the way I have nurtured a small talent for writing fiction and criticism, a talent which has yielded me fewer results than I would have anticipated but much pleasure. My own effort to write something meaningful and not clichéd, something my own in some way connected to the human spirit, has furnished me with a large and healthy respect for Texas writers whose originality must deal with and transcend the mythology of the territory and contend with a dynamism and diversity that make being a "New York writer" by comparison as natural as loving the

---

This essay was written especially for the present volume.

Brooklyn Bridge. I have, I suppose, been a member of the Republic of Texas Letters since the publication of my first novel in 1961, and I have had some part in its structure. The Res or Idea I keep primarily in my mind about it is something that has been important and meaningful, often sustaining, to me as I have lived and worked these many years in Texas, and that is the strong, clear, shared notion of fellowship.

This idea was ingrained in me early by my colleague, friend, and mentor Lon Tinkle, a thoroughly civilized person whose contribution to Texas letters has never been fully appreciated. Maybe that is because he was associated with Dallas during the time when Dallas was associated in people's minds with image-mongering, "selling the sizzle not the steak." There was plenty of sizzle to Lon, and indeed he did love image, loved to gild whatever lily was at hand. I have even heard Lon gild a cactus. However that may be, Lon Tinkle reviewed and encouraged more young Texas writing talent than any other figure ever on the state's literary scene. He was our respected representative to the national literary scene and was leader and inspirer of a circle of civilized literary people in Dallas who shared his genuine concern for the creative spirit, good writing, and the encouragement of individual writers.

Young Larry McMurtry, in an essay famous among us in his *In a Narrow Grave,* published in 1968, made fun of Lon Tinkle for declaiming at a boring meeting of the Texas Institute of Letters at the old Driskill Hotel in Austin that the TIL could and should be a kind of French Academy, when it was nothing but a club of regional writers. Granted that *In a Narrow Grave* was a valuable book, in which McMurtry, representing a new literary generation and the first to be serious about the novel and poetry in Texas, was the Young Bull taking on the Old Bulls, and the old bullshit, but the mockery of Tinkle was misapplied. I keep the image from that essay of McMurtry watching old J. Frank Dobie toiling up the street in the heat in Austin and letting him pass without speaking to him, not taking him as a real man or fellow writer but as a passing Myth, thinking of him as "one of the Old Ones of this land [who] will soon be gone, no more to ride the river nor follow the Longhorn cow." This essay did a stimulating job of taking on the Establishment and clearing the brush, but the hazard is always that you end up beating on the only forces at work for what you yourself believe in. What Tinkle was speaking for was objectivity in judging literary talent and for a sense of critical and spiritual community among the writers in the state, or anyway among those who accepted membership in a group such as the Texas Institute of Letters. Twenty years later, first in his *Texas Observer* essay and then in his travels around the state following the success of *Lonesome Dove,* a good-spirited Larry McMurtry has been advocating an objectivity and encouragement of the fellowship of writers very similar to what Lon Tinkle had in mind.

Gallic and cosmopolitan in looks, wit, and intelligence, a professor of French and of comparative literature, Tinkle grew up in Dallas's Oak Cliff and had his literary roots in the workshop of Southern Methodist University's legendary John Hathaway McGinnis, who brought distinction to the SMU Press, *Southwest Review,* and the *Dallas Morning News* book page. (My own Texas literary roots go back to this tradition.) For forty years, then, Lon Tinkle performed in his columns in the *Morning News* a tough act, a kind of double whammy indigenous and necessary to frontier communities not used to criticism of anything, let alone art. He both encouraged and served as evaluative critic to Texas writers.

This kind of work was evolutionary. One had to encourage the buds and not bruise them, and at the same time to give them some sense of their place in their immediate garden and also in the larger garden. And Tinkle was virtually the only critic of Texas literature in the state during his lifetime. I think it may be correct to say that true criticism of Texas fiction and poetry only just began with the insightful remarks of R. G.

Vliet during the conference on the Texas Literary Tradition held at the University of Texas at Austin in 1983. The next step for Texas literature is to make criticism of Texas writing not personal opinion and not sociological or folkloric, but a literary discipline.

Now that most of the sham controversies and obvious anomalies having to do with Texas as a "nation" and as a state and its regions and regionalisms have been smoked out and cleared away, we should be better able to greet lit as lit and not as a function of something else. I see Lon Tinkle and his life-long balancing act as right at the fulcrum of this teeter-totter between the blind provincialism of the past and the new spirit of criticism in Texas.

Tinkle, who gave me my sense of the fellowship among authors, had among his other distinctive qualities those of an impresario, a showman of literature without equal before or since in our state. Part of this gift he exercised in bringing in nationally recognized writers as models to us provincials. How often he would seat "Red" Warren or Paul Horgan at the top of a circle of us and beam at the prospect of the dialectic that was sure to ensue! He brought Katherine Anne Porter to us in Dallas. (And his lovely wife Maria laundered Miss Porter's nightgowns by hand when Katherine Anne got sick and repaired to a hospital for a spell.) No matter her pique and our shame that Dobie got the TIL award for best book back in 1939, Katherine Anne Porter never held it against Lon Tinkle, whom she heartily liked. He nearly singlehandedly redeemed Texas to her. She had no doubt, nor do I, that Lon would have given her the award, for *Pale Horse, Pale Rider,* and for her style and panache.

Lon's greatest piece of showmanship was bringing T. S. Eliot to Texas in March of 1959. He saw the poet, who was seventy then and just remarried, in London and invited him over, promising him a fee of some five thousand dollars. In the moment of the offer he had no idea where the sum would come from, but he raised it and cut a deal to bring Eliot first to the University of Texas in Austin and then to SMU. Brimming with confidence, Lon booked the poet into the mammoth new red-and-blue-seated Moody Coliseum at SMU. I remember going there with Lon thinking the setting would be more appropriate for a match between the Christians and the lions than for T. S. Eliot. I think Lon's heart sank a little too as he surveyed the vast arena, with its tiers of ten thousand seats above the basketball court. We put five hundred chairs on a tarp down on the floor so as not to be embarrassed too badly if just a few showed up. The night came, the blackest, rainiest, blowiest night I had ever seen on the prairie. And from several surrounding states and all over Texas came more than nine thousand people of all ages to hear the poet read from his work. I could have wept for joy. Lon sat calmly at our little table on the floor before the podium, stroking his mustache, and at a certain point suggested I get the poet a glass of water, which I carried up to him in the guise of Gunga Din. Lon was terribly pleased. The success of the reading made up for the reporter who, upon Mr. Eliot's arrival at Love Field, had asked him what was the name of his poem about the wasteland.

On that occasion I met a fellow named A. C. Greene who had come over from his bookshop in Abilene to hear and meet the poet and who would later name a son for him. Soon thereafter Greene came to Dallas, and, as we should never forget, was the courageous and wise editorial editor of the *Dallas Times Herald*, a sane voice during the confusion and hysteria following the Kennedy assassination. Later, he became book editor. From the first, A. C. Greene was, like Tinkle, a keen encourager of Texas writing. He reviewed both my novels of the sixties and was kind to *Tom Northway*, which struck a chord in him. His wonderful *A Personal Country* and his *Highland Park Woman* struck chords in me. Through the years we developed the kind of personal-professional relationship that comes from mutual respect and attention to intentions. This kind of relationship, morticed with the respect for the written work, is what holds the house of letters together in any state or nation, or, as PEN knows, in the world. I count now on those friendships with writers younger than myself that developed from my early reading of their work: Shelby Hearon's *Armadillo in the Grass* and *Hannah's House,* C. W. Smith's *Thin Men of Haddam* and *Country Music,* Laura Furman's "Eldorado" and *The Glass House,* Jack Myers's *The Family War,* Stephen Harrigan's *Aransas,* and so on, as well as the older writers who have been my mentors and my friends.

To use academic terms of which they would not approve, A. C. Greene is our present dean in charge of the definition of "Texas literature" (and Larry McMurtry has resigned as the *enfant terrible* dean of the rival school), while the honorable John Graves is our much respected and heeded dean for literary merit, our Dean of Integrity, if you will.

Graves's reputation in Texas is built on his fine writing, his *sui generis* work, and also upon the respect in which we hold him. He is the most singular and solitary of well-known Texas literary figures yet also has perhaps the deepest sense of community. He has inspired among us a kind of shared commitment to what is good and is or may be—if we're damn careful and don't let it roll back on us—true.

A loner, sitting over there in Somervell County on hardscrabble, Graves is terribly important to us because of his Virgilian wisdom and particularity of knowledge, his inheritance of the mantle of tough individuality enacted in the old context of tough Nature from Bedichek and Dobie, and because he is characteristically—shy, sensitive, eye cocked and mind running deep as a river with clear springs at the source—so forthcoming in sharing his mind with us. Graves is a genuine talent, and no writer in America feels more deeply the lonely difficulty of the work of writing and the need for occasional understanding companionship along the way of this (speaking metaphorically) long and quixotic "running of the buffalo."

A stylistically elegant writer, his work indeed harking back to the themes and concerns of Virgil's *Georgics,* that didactic poem on the cultivation of the soil and the rearing of cattle and bees, John Graves is low-key in person, in public speaking as in private conversation. Most of us know very few whole human beings, and we notice about each that his or her persona is almost one with his or her true self. So it is with Graves. He is who he is but there is just a slight ironic edge to him that, mostly playfully, warns you against taking too seriously what an "old crock" (his term) like himself might utter. And the best things I have heard him utter, yea, like crocks of much fine gold, as he spoke under the tough old trees at Mr. Webb's Friday Mountain, have had to do with the paradox of effort and result in writing and the necessity of understanding and community among those fools of the spirit who seriously and for the long running undertake it.

All this may sound a bit on the high and tender side, and I can see some of the more acerbic cowboys in Texas crunching ice wisely and figuring that old Terry has begun his descent into dottiness. But if you take all the individual effort and the time and the trials and errors of writing, all the gold words and the words of lead and the tinkling brass and symbols, all the early hopes and visions and conceptions and their results, you have got to add at least a dollop from the crock of community of effort and support, or crack. We are lucky to have had this idea of the worth of writing, this shared idea, in Texas; to have had it for many years before the host of new writers, in universities or whatever, arrived, and to have it still. It is not just in institutions, say the TIL or the Texas Association of Creative Writing Teachers, though it is certainly in them and among those not in both organizations, or in neither, or in none. Praise God that it sanely transcends the organizations. I think we can call it a Res or Idea because, in Plato's sense, it precedes and defines *a priori* and essentially those of us who are serious about writing and have worked at it. It is an intangible but very real recognition in and for each individual writer that she or he is part of something, and that that thing is good. It's a recognition of values shared.

I keep in my mind, in regard to all this, the TIL meeting of a few years ago when Max Apple received an award. After accepting, Max paused a moment and looked around. Then he said, "At these meetings we spend a lot of time asking why the TIL exists. I like to come together once a year to see friends who are writers and meet others. I don't think we need always to be asking why. We know why."

I am sitting writing this in a room which looks out over the Fellows Garden of University College, by charter from William of Durham the oldest Oxford college. As the slant of evening sun turns the mellow stone and spires of these sixteenth-century buildings to gold and Great Tom nearby begins to toll, I think I know how J. Frank Dobie felt as he held his experience and sense of life and literature up to the long perspective of Cambridge. Shakespeare, Dobie said, was his idea of a great regionalist; but he knew that he himself carried the burden of creating a literature—the lore and history put into words—of his own scarcely defined and unwritten country. What Dobie was to take part in doing was what many American writers have done as civilization moved west over our continent. As the teacher Cleric, in *My Ántonia,* quotes to Jim Burden, from Virgil, "Primus ego in patriam mecum . . . deducam Musas"; "for I shall be the first, if I live, to bring the Muse into my country."

The fact that Katherine Anne Porter thought and declared that *she* was decidedly the first to deal with any true Muse having to do with Texas only sparks the fire that lights up our double tradition of writing in Texas, or what we might call Big Two-Hearted Tex Lit: that we do indeed have a rich background and present industry of both folkloric-historical and "literary" writing. The old mythology so brilliantly described years ago by Henry Nash Smith in *Virgin Land,* the Myth of the West as sustaining belief and force in history and in the creative imagination, threads through both tiers of work. The Texas historians and the journalists, therefore, generally have maintained that there is a full-fledged "Texas literature" composed of fiction and nonfiction that is quite like a nation's literature in that it is the chronicle and record of a large and diverse region that became a state after it had in fact been a nation and that remains a potent symbol of freedom, individuality, and Social Darwinism to the rest of the United States and to the world. On the other hand, most poets and fiction writers in Texas and beyond its borders maintain that by measure of quality there is no "Texas literature" as such but just a diverse bunch of writers at work writing some good stuff and some bad stuff.

I myself am of both minds. That is because both contentions are true.

The truth that all of us great writers and critics and scholars of Tex Lit know and love to obfuscate is that "Texas literature" both is and is not, philosophically un-Greeklike as that notion is. It's no Nobel shakes so far in purely literary terms, but in sheer weight and heft, hide and horn, bale and boll, lore and earnest recounting, it's a lot.

Texas thinkers and writers have been knowing that for a long time, actually, at least for the twenty-five or more years that I have beheld the Texas scene professionally. For example, nobody understood the older tradition of historical reality, frontier myth, and regionalism better than Lon Tinkle. Yet the last significant word of his career as interpreter of Texas literature was to tell us, at the Texas Institute of Letters meeting in 1977, that we must turn to the celebration of "not 'regionalism,' but the artist in our midst." Nonetheless for the last decade or so we have all had a jolly time eating hoecakes and drinking fern-bar wine,* that is to say, confusing the issue, with all the gusto of a walk-down between John Wayne and Chevy Chase on the set of *The Alamo* at Brackettville.

These "controversies" have in fact been pretty lively and interesting, if not chock-full of content. They have been more poses, that is, one pose opposing another pose until we slumber off into blissful equipoise.

The great hoorah over whether Texas indeed has or should have a national literature probably resulted from our somewhat pretentious if always truly well-intended setup of a state writers' organization that gives healthy prizes for "Texas" work, encourages writers through fellowships to live and write at Dobie's old ranch Paisano, and in general manages to give the impression year to year that there is something to toot about writin'-wise in Texas, no matter what might be the backward state of literary affairs in Idaho, Alaska, or Connecticut. On top of that, every few years here came favorite son Larry McMurtry on a visit back to Texas to survey the scene from a perspective he could not imagine most of us already possessed. On these inspection visits McMurtry, from time to time, informed us that Texas was now an urban state and writers should pay attention to that, as he did so well in his own "Houston trilogy," and that stories about young Ronnie Bob coming off the ranch or farm and making his way into the new frontier of the city had just about been done. At any rate, we must never, never inflict another Texas trail-driving saga on our readers!

Also, then, McMurtry tried to get us in Texas not to be so pretentious, and he did this, in his famous *Texas Observer* essay, by means of a catalogue of good and bad and some pretty

---

*"Won't we have a jolly time, eating cakes and drinking wine . . . at the Golden Wedding. . . ." Old song sung to me by Tom Northway when I was a boy, also in fragment form in Joyce's *Ulysses.*

stern—or humorous, whichever you will—definitions of what it is to be a "Texas writer" that harked more to the botanist's view of life and work than the literary critic's. He did manage to rout from our sugarplum heads any notion that Flauberts or Henry Jameses or Willa Cathers were in any good supply among us, before jump-shifting from total prose assessment to his well-taken accolade for one of the few poets who has ever as a native practiced the craft in Texas. I myself was delighted to be included in a list of writers of traditional narrative and was only amazed that McMurtry's overall assessment came as big news, or could possibly be thought controversial by anyone. But of course much of Texas's famous ego, that shield of seeming superiority, has to do with frontier insecurity, and this detailed botanical labeling was taken by some to be an attack on Texas.

It is interesting to step aside for a moment and reflect that Dobie's throwing-in with the Texas Institute of Letters, agreeing to by God be a part of such an organization, was an assertion in that Centennial year that literature and such were important, and should be noted, at a time when Texans were excited about just about everything in their past and present *except* literature. And those founders of the TIL fifty years ago did set in motion a literary engine, a literary machine bigger and better than that in any other state, which has run, thank you, on a quantity of pride and even pomposity through the years.

A. C. Greene had also been pondering these matters, and in one way or the other the issue was joined between him and McMurtry.

Greene had always been tuned to Texas writing and its various purposes and its roots in the experience of Texans from the first settlers to now. It was not Greene's position, as I understand it, that such an entity as "Texas literature" needed defending for quantity or quality, or that it was the greatest stuff ever scribbled on foolscap or scrawled on rawhide, but simply that there was indeed a significant body of work that related to Texas in Texas's literal, historical, and mythical dimensions that deserved to be pointed to and remembered and that on the whole it made a distinctive body of work.

Greene produced a little volume called *The Fifty Best Books on Texas,* as admirable for its knowledge of the scope of writing about Texas as for its objectivity of choices, and charmingly quirky in its rationalizations for the choices. The first thing he says is that these are books *about* Texas, maybe not the best-written books by Texans, whatever in the world we might finally rule Texans to be. (Greene himself had a good story about this dilemma. When I first got to know him he told me of being a reporter in Abilene when the editor called a meeting about an obituary which declared that a person had been a native of Abilene for twenty-five years. As I recall, they changed the tenure to thirty.) At any rate, what Greene was doing was valuable catalogue-wise and was straightforward enough so that he had no qualms about blasting big-bore through logical-critical qualifications: ". . . they may not be the most important Texas books—but don't let's get off into a thicket of objections and explanations: the quality of the books speaks for itself. They are the best."

And sure enough, it makes a good list, particularly in its nonfiction component, a list which I take affirms my earlier point about there being a historical-sociological-folkloric treasurehouse of Texas stuff. From *Coronado's Children* to *Charles Goodnight* and *13 Days to Glory* and *Adventures with a Texas Naturalist* to *Six Years with the Texas Rangers* and *Goodbye to a River* it is a rich record of a territory, nation, state, and state of mind that Texas schoolchildren study and grow up thinking is absolutely special and that Europeans still think of as a nation. Of the fiction entries there are no immortal works, unless you count *Pale Horse, Pale Rider* as truly significant in American

literature. The other novels and stories are interesting as curi-
osities, especially to those readers fascinated by Texas, as, say,
lyrical evocations of youth in a non-lyrical place, or as true
historical records of a time past, or, in the case of *Sironia,
Texas,* just for being so doggedly persistent in the telling.

So anyway, for a while there everyone was polishing his
Bowie knife and practicing his draw and hoping that in the
forums that popped up to elucidate these issues all hell would
break loose, that the great antagonists McMurtry and Greene
would confront if not confound each other. This was due to
the mistaken notion that they were at odds, which seemed to
the general onlooker to be the case as McMurtry was attacking
Texas literature as a great disappointment to him personally
and Greene seemed to be intent on defending its substance.
Actually, of course, they were banded together in the belief or
hope that by God there was or should be a "Texas literature."
They were, hi-ever, raising a lot of dust, and most kindhearted
lit folks in Texas as well as a scattering of the public naturally
cherished the idea that they would savagely shout at each
other at one of these forums, and maybe one would manage to
damage the other's head severely with the water pitcher.

I know that I was pretty excited when McMurtry came to
read from a work in progress called *Lonesome Dove* at the tenth
anniversary of the SMU Literary Festival, for I had also invited A. C. Greene to the dinner before the reading. I made
my way through the throng of students, professors, and an
unsuspecting poet or two from far places in my living room to
my back porch and lo! there were the two antagonists seated
side by side, Greene making that slow, sage motion of his
head that means he is about to say something, McMurtry
poker-faced as Amarillo Slim, poised for battle. I hastened to
the table and sat by them.

"Larry, do you remember that old man in Ranger, he had
that huge library in his house up there on that hill?" A. C. said.

"Yes," Larry said. "I have often wondered what happened to him and to those books."

This is not to say that these so-called controversies are irrelevant. They are quite relevant to those who chronicle the play of issues literary in Texas. They are just irrelevant to individual writers.

The other controversy that perennially ripples up and ruffles feelings in the writing community in the state is over membership in the Texas Institute of Letters. After I published my first book I was informed sternly that no one was elected to membership in the TIL without two books, and I believed it, though I did notice quite a few exceptions. Seven years later I became a member and very quickly found myself on the Council of the organization and, following Bill Wittliff, became one of two very young presidents, given the precedents. Since then I have grown hoary in the service of the TIL as councillor and judge. I think that the Council over the past decade has done a good job of making the organization less chauvinistic, both in the sense of maleness and parochialism; of opening up and broadening out the membership to reflect the real literary scene in Texas; and of enriching the prizes and stabilizing the base of the Dobie-Paisano Fellowship, through which so many promising, mostly young, Texas writers have had a rare opportunity to get their writing done.

Having been so close to it, I am happy to be able to set a few things straight about the TIL.

It is true that in my early days on the Council Jack Daniel's was reported as present and rapidly diminishing, and that the procedures were somewhat informal, especially as to membership choice. I missed Mr. Dobie, but the likes of Holland McCombs, Paul Baker, Lon Tinkle, Frank Wardlaw, Wilson Hudson, Harry Ransom, Martin Shockley, as well as Greene, Graves, and Wittliff, could be found in attendance, with some of the memorable meetings being at Greene's San Cristóbal or at the nearby Paisano. It was quite a breakthrough when

THE REPUBLIC OF TEXAS LETTERS

Shelby Hearon joined the Council, drank her whiskey straight, and became the first contemporary woman president. I recall that potential members were almost always judged for literary merit of their work, though sometimes that was done arbitrarily. One time, for example, a fairly prominent author's name was raised to a reaction around the room of general silence on the part of the councillors. "Well, why not?" his proponent said, looking around the room. "He has written a half-dozen books, which is more than can be said for most of us." Silence. (In those days a turn of the head, a spit to the side, or a cock of the eye could be taken for an answer. The older Texans believed in sign and did not like to speak out against anybody overtly.) When the proponent pressed it one more time, he got an overt answer from one of the Old Ones, who declared, "The son of a bitch don't write good." Since then, the criteria for membership have been strengthened, articulated, and re-articulated and the debate over new members has become sophisticated and precise in the TIL Council.

To the charge that real Texans are left out of membership in the TIL while any New Yorker who crosses the border is hustled in, I can only say that since I am in Dallas I was assigned the task of apprehending visiting Eastern writers at DFW Airport. In my zeal to rope these outlanders and sizzle the TIL brand on them, I must ruefully confess to making some mistakes, especially in my eagerness to grab deplaning New York poets. These mistakes resulted in the TIL's taking in a haberdasher, an MGM stuntman, three evangelists, and a nuclear physicist due quite simply to my inability to recognize a New York poet when I saw one; and I am sure that those Council members stationed to watch the airports in Houston and Austin have made similar mistakes.

The most fun I have had recently in regard to "regionalism" was at the spring '87 meeting of the national Associated Writing Programs at where else but the old-new Driskill Hotel in Austin. They had a lot of panels, and of course asked some Texas writers to do a panel on regionalism. What else, if you were having a national meeting of writers and writing teachers in Texas, would you ask the Texas writers to talk about than regionalism? Anyway, on this panel the poet Cynthia Macdonald spoke of the vitality of writing in Houston brought by the writers coming from out of state to teach at the university. Though not my own, that was an interesting view. Certainly it is a valid idea that as the oligarchies of the great Renaissance cities of Europe created centers for artists to flourish in so are our universities those patrons now. Yet it would be my bet that a society in as much ferment as Texas would produce from its own roots and soil its own distinctive writers, and particularly black and Chicano poets and novelists to fill in the straight of Texas writing. (Texas has certainly done so in recent years with the blooming of Rolando Hinojosa, Rosemary Catacalos, Naomi Shihab Nye, Pat Mora, Harryette Mullen, and others.) My deep belief is that a culture does yeast up its own creative talent.

I liked what James Hoggard, a Texas multi-talent, said on that same panel. It ties back in with the theme of writerly fellowship with which I began. Talking about the writers and publishers and other literary folk in Texas, he said, "The people we're referring to are the passionate few who keep the candles lit. They began in many quarters and came here: some recently, some a long time back. But they've set their torches here, and they're mindful of the large and small sides of their own culture, and they get to know other writers whose work they often read, translate, and publish. The people we're concerned with continue learning, and they speak in many voices, though the Southwestern voice, one learns, is often subtle. . . ."

After the panel, which we joyously declared to be the last panel on regionalism that any Texas writer would ever participate in, Hoggard and the fine Texas writer Bryan Woolley and I repaired to the lobby and ordered two regional and one national beers and put one pair of regional-Texas, one pair of regional-Maine, and one pair of national-brand-name feet on the table. Every once in a while somebody would go by about whom Woolley would pass the comment, "Looks like a regional to me." Then I walked out into a gorgeous Texas midday with the bluest sky and walked up to the Capitol and renewed acquaintance with the Terry Texas Ranger and walked back down and sat on the curb with several hundred other people to watch a big equestrian parade come up the street. And here came phalanxes of beautiful horses of all kinds, prancing by with their prideful riders young and old all in hats and chaps and proper boots, and then here came the Shriners in their fezzes in their little go-carts just a-zipping through what the horses had dropped, making figure eights through it, and the crowd laughing and applauding, the beauty of the horses and the affectation and pride of the parade both appreciated and mocked, and the sun was shining in that wondrous blue sky and a whole cartful of balloons let go from a balloon-man's cart, and the Shriners zipped on down the street scattering the horsestuff far and wee, and I felt in that moment more Texan than I ever really have been. I felt right Texian.

Way back there in 1936, at the time of the founding of the Texas Institute of Letters, J. Frank Dobie said: "Great literature transcends its native land, but there is none I know of that ignores its own soil. All great literature plumbs and soars to the elementals—Texas authors need not be antiquarian; in the rich soil of the novel there has not been even a furrow plowed."

So it remains, though in the novel furrows have been plowed. Larry McMurtry has plowed a furrow in the novel. Young, he realized that Dobie, Webb, and Bedichek, while being wonderful examples of staying true to values, did not prepare the way for the forms of creative writing they did not really understand. Now McMurtry has become for Texas the middleman between the Triad and the present. And writing will go on, with much diversity, in and out of universities, by occasionals and professionals, regionals and peripatetics and whomever, those both aware and unaware of these traditions and questions about writing and writers and the canon of literature associated with Texas. As far as I know I will be for the most part physically in Texas, writing, though probably as often in Ohio or England or Spain or New Mexico in my head. Meanwhile that bond, that Res of fellowship that embraces our Republic of Letters will sustain those writers of good faith and true intention.

HERDING WORDS: TEXAS LITERATURE AS TRAIL DRIVE

Tom Pilkington

> I grew up in a herding tradition and that's determined
> everything I've done. I was never good at herding cattle,
> but writing is a way of herding words . . . and I suspect
> by my constant driving around the country I'm prac-
> ticing a form of trail-driving. . . .
> —Larry McMurtry, *New York Times,* 9 June 1985

When it first began to enter my consciousness, roughly a
quarter-century ago, that my own, my native state had produced some writers who were worth reading, those writers at
the time were ordinarily thought of as Southwestern writers
rather than as Texas writers. In fact, one critic, Lawrence
Clark Powell, a Southern Californian who believed himself to
be a Southwesterner, in the late 1950s conferred upon that
arch-Texan J. Frank Dobie the title "Mr. Southwest." This act
was no doubt performed in public acknowledgment of Dobie's
mostly successful campaign, a life-long endeavor, to associate
Texas with the Southwest—that vast region stretching from
West Texas to California—rather than with the South. At any
rate, in the 1950s and 1960s, and well into the 1970s, most bibliographies, literary histories, anthologies, and other reference

---

The first version of this essay was delivered as an address at the 1984 Symposium on the Humanities sponsored by the Texas Committee for the
Humanities and held in Austin, Texas. In 1986 the address was substantially revised and given as a talk at several events honoring the Texas Sesquicentennial. It is published here with minor additional revisions.

tools of the sort that dealt with Texas writers at all considered them as part of a larger regional culture—that is, the culture of the Southwest. Today, fewer people speak of Texas writers as contributors to Southwestern literature; most employ, almost automatically, the phrase "Texas literature."

An example of this shift comes from the nonfiction of the state's best-known living writer, Larry McMurtry. McMurtry's 1968 collection, *In a Narrow Grave: Essays on Texas,* contains a chapter called "Southwestern Literature?" In that essay McMurtry talks mostly about Texas writers—but don't overlook the word *Southwestern* in the title of the piece. Thirteen years later, in 1981—23 October 1981, to be precise—McMurtry's iconoclastic article "Ever a Bridegroom: Reflections on the Failure of Texas Literature" appeared in the *Texas Observer.* It was a shot heard 'round Texas—maybe even 'round the world—and McMurtry's contention that Texas literature has been, to this point, a dismal "failure" detonated an explosive controversy, with charges and countercharges ricocheting through the state's literary circles. I will not comment on the controversy here, except to say that it has not died out completely to this day (witness the many references to it in this volume). To me one of the most interesting things about McMurtry's *Observer* essay is that it assumes, unlike the 1968 piece, that there *is* a recognizable body of writing that we may call "Texas literature," failed though the author believes it to be.

Further evidence of the triumph of the concept of a separate and distinct Texas literature came in the form of a gaudy, three-day symposium on the Texas Literary Tradition, held in Austin in March 1983 and sponsored by the University of Texas. Three years later, in September 1986, in Denton, North Texas State University put on a shindig which bore the imprimatur of the governor's office and was called "Texas Images and Realities: The Governor's Sesquicentennial Conference on the Literary Arts." Audiences totaling well over a thousand people attended each of these conferences, and both the Austin and Denton get-togethers were covered by all the state's major newspapers, as well as by some out-of-state papers.

A citizen of, say, North Dakota or Kansas might well find such symposia passing strange. North Dakotans do not claim for themselves a North Dakota literature, nor do Kansans normally think in terms of a Kansas "literary tradition." North Dakota and Kansas writing is considered—if it is considered at all—as Texas writing used to be, as part of a more encompassing regional literature. Furthermore, people from other states may think the idea of a Texas Institute of Letters rather pretentious. The TIL was founded in 1936, during the state's Centennial celebration, to be a select body charged with fostering in Texas the creative act of writing and the critical appreciation of that writing. But a state having its own institute of letters strikes some as absurd—European rather than American—and down through the years there have been those, including Larry McMurtry at one time (recently McMurtry has become an active member of the TIL), who have chided both the theory and practice of the organization. Again, what other state has its own institute of letters?

It is easy, then, to poke fun at the concept of a uniquely Texan literature, just as it is easy to ridicule the "Texas mystique" in its varied and sometimes ludicrous manifestations. But the idea of a Texas literary tradition, to me, does make a good deal of sense. Certainly I have written much over the years that begins with the assumption that such a tradition exists. Larry Swindell, book-page editor of the *Fort Worth Star-Telegram,* contributed an article to the *Washington Post Book World* some time back which suggested a practical rationale for entertaining such a premise. Texas, Swindell said, is a widely recognized brand name in literature, thanks to the universal currency of "the Texas mystique and the Texas myth." Americans in general and Texans in particular buy books about Texas—lots of them.

Book people—who, if they are successful, are also hard-headed business people—are aware of the attitude Swindell was trying to describe. Is there a bookstore in the state that does not sport a lavishly stocked and prominently displayed "Texana" section? National publishers often court Texas au-thors, because of their sales potential, while largely ignoring those from Wisconsin or Idaho. Moreover, as Swindell pointed out, a lively publishing industry, comprising both commercial and university presses, now flourishes within Texas. "What is currently happening in Texas," Swindell concluded, "couldn't happen in any other state, not even in California. . . . Even if they don't realize it, there are many whose heartbeats define them as Texans first and Americans second. Somehow this translates into a national broad base for Texas books. . . ."

Swindell may have been wrong about California—there is a movement afoot in that state to promote what is termed "California literature"—but he was essentially correct. Most Texans do think of themselves as part of a separate and dis-tinct entity. Of the states of the union Texas is uniquely, to adopt a phrase apparently coined in 1915 by Zane Grey in his popular novel *The Lone Star Ranger,* "a world in itself." (Many a writer since, including George Sessions Perry in his 1942 volume *Texas: A World in Itself,* has perpetuated the cliché.) Or, as historian T. R. Fehrenbach asserts, it is a "nation-state." One of the advantages of employing Texas as a means of cate-gorizing works of literature is that it is a well-defined geo-graphical unit. We can look on a map—as we cannot in the case of a nebulous region such as the Southwest—and see its boundaries clearly outlined. Within those borders Texas pos-sesses more topographical, ethnic, and cultural diversity than do most of the nations of the world. And yet it is held together by a powerful, chauvinistic mythology that generates fierce loyalty from almost all who think of themselves as Texans. It seems to me, therefore, that the idea of a "Texas literature" is as justifiable—and, again, as subject to ridicule—as the idea of Texas music, Texas cooking, Texas clothing, or, most grandiose of all, a Texas lifestyle.

Having said as much, let me proceed to assert—well, I guess A. C. Greene and Larry McMurtry said this quite a while ago—the importance of pausing occasionally to take stock, to consider Texas writing within the context of other literatures and other cultures. It is all too easy to forget that Texas literature is only a small and, many would say, relatively insignificant part of American literature, of Western European literature, and of world literature. John Graves is on target when he warns, as he did in a recent interview, that Texas literature "is just a segment of the whole and has to stand ultimately on how well it stacks up against writing from N.Y.C. or Minnesota or whatever." What Graves is talking about here is the question of quality. Just how good is Texas writing? Is literary Texas an empire or a banana republic?

That there may be bad Texas books as well as good Texas books is a thought that probably never occurs to Texans who think about books at all. For Texans, Texas books—like Texas cattle, Texas oil (what's left of it), and Texas bidness— are, in and of themselves, good because they are Texan. I know several people, fellow Texans all, who own near-complete sets of the works of the aforementioned J. Frank Dobie. Dobie's books sit on shelves beside volumes by Louis L'Amour and Stephen King. These folks read Louis L'Amour and Stephen King; they do not, for the most part, read Dobie. Nonetheless Dobie is revered by many Texans. He taught Texans how to succeed at the culture game. He gave Texans a literary identity at a time when foreigners, i.e., people living outside the state, refused to acknowledge there was such a thing as Texas writing—or even Southwestern writing. Thus Dobie is seen as a natural resource, as important on the cultural level as cattle, cotton, and oil are—or were—on the economic level.

Obviously we need to be more critical in our approach to Texas literature than this naive, chauvinistic reaction allows. And without a doubt evaluations of Texas writing in the 1980s have been more penetrating and, one hopes, more sophisticated than they ever were in the past. Beginning in the late 1970s and early 1980s, A. C. Greene wrote several articles and essays that are largely responsible for initiating the lively discussions of Texas writing that have punctuated the eighties. For example, Greene's "The Fifty Best Texas Books" appeared in the August 1981 issue of *Texas Monthly*. This list, later fleshed out and put between hard covers under the title *The Fifty Best Books on Texas,* seems in retrospect to have been offered with a kind of good-natured innocence. Greene did not make any extravagant claims for the books included in his catalogue; he simply said, Here are some good Texas books worthy of a serious reader's attention. As a matter of fact, in *The Fifty Best* (the book, not the article), Greene had the audacity—and the honesty?—to compare Texas writing with New Mexico writing and to find Lone Star letters clearly lacking: "Texas," he adjudged, "has not furnished indigenous materials for great novels " such as those by Oliver La Farge, Frank Waters, and Adolph Bandelier. "It has drawn out no *Death Comes for the Archbishop,* and few products comparable to Richard Bradford's *Red Sky at Morning.*"

Interestingly, the fact that Texas writing was about to take a bashing was signaled by the appearance of a piece by Gregory Curtis, a former student of Larry McMurtry's at Rice University and editor of *Texas Monthly,* in the same August 1981 issue of the magazine that carried Greene's "The Fifty Best Texas Books." Writing in his "Behind the Lines" column, Curtis proclaimed that "the curse of Texas letters is that for the most part our hallowed writers are themselves more interesting than their books." This statement was followed by a thorough flaying of the hapless (and deceased) J. Frank Dobie and his disciples. Though he professed to admire the work of a bare handful of contemporary Texas writers, Curtis concluded that few of the state's authors have contributed literature that has "practical value"—that is to say, books that "tell us who we are now and who our ancestors were then."

Hard on the heels of the August 1981 *Texas Monthly* came the *Texas Observer* which contained McMurtry's "Ever a Bridegroom." This soon-to-be notorious issue hit the streets with a bang in October 1981. As the subtitle of McMurtry's piece indicates, he believed (and presumably still believes, given his 1987 postscript to the essay) that Texas literature has been an irredeemable failure. A sizable boatload of critics and commentators, writers and reporters has bobbed in the choppy wake of Greene and McMurtry, and throughout the 1980s the subject of the quality of Texas writing has been debated in the pages of magazines and newspapers, from platforms and podiums across the state. A great deal of heat has been generated, and now and then a few glimmerings of light have been shed upon the topic.

It seems to me that Texas literature is still a very young literature and that Texas, as a literary entity, has not really had an opportunity yet either to succeed *or* to fail. Texas's literary development appears to be following the larger pattern of American literary development. American literature, we must recall, has not always enjoyed its current lofty status as one of the world's great literatures. In the eighteenth and well into the nineteenth centuries, American writing was dismissed by Europeans as embarrassingly provincial and immature. American artists and intellectuals were very much aware of this attitude and were stung by the barbs of snooty critics such as the

Englishman Sydney Smith, who wrote an infamous essay in 1819 for the *Edinburgh Review:* "In the four quarters of the globe," Smith asked, "who reads an American book? or goes to an American play? or looks at an American picture?"

In the early and middle decades of the nineteenth century many American writers, including William Cullen Bryant, William Gilmore Simms, Herman Melville, and, most notable of all, Ralph Waldo Emerson—whose "The American Scholar" address in 1837 came to be widely known as America's "intellectual declaration of independence"—published strident, chauvinistic proclamations calling for American writers to break free of the chains of European cultural domination and to forge a uniquely American civilization and culture. These proclamations were no doubt prompted as much by anxiety and a nagging fear of inferiority as they were by confident expectation. But fortunately for American writing the talent that rescued these statements from the realm of windy rhetoric began to appear in the middle part of the nineteenth century.

Even so it took a long time for American literature to be accorded its rightful status and respect. In the latter half of the nineteenth century Henry James, an American soon to become a European, could still lament that the American scene was not conducive to the artistic temperament because it contained "no castles . . . no ivied ruins"—in effect, no culture worthy of the name. Throughout the twentieth century, writers and other artists have continued to complain about the crassness, the materialism, the violence of American society. What they have often overlooked is the vitality of that society—a vitality that has fueled a remarkable proliferation of the arts in our time, just as it has fueled unprecedented economic growth. Though America may be, as some have suggested, currently in a state of literary decadence—its literary batteries having run down parallel to the entropic decline of its industrial machine—a glimpse back over the past century and more of American writing reveals a grand and glorious record, an inventory of literary accomplishments that owe much of their power to the very crassness, materialism, and violence of the society from which they have issued.

Texas writers, therefore, can draw strength from the examples of earlier American writers and their sometimes painful struggle to be taken seriously. Most cogently, however, they can look for aesthetic inspiration to the recent literary history of a neighboring province. I refer to the so-called "Southern Renaissance." As late as 1917 H. L. Mencken contended, in his essay "The Sahara of the Bozart," that the American South was "as sterile, artistically, intellectually, culturally, as the Sahara Desert." Aside from James Branch Cabell, Mencken said, "you will not find a single Southern prose writer who can actually write. . . . [The South] has no art, no literature, no philosophy, no mind or aspiration of her own." It is as if Southern writers, Faulkner and the Agrarians among others, were lying in wait to ambush the reckless Mencken, for the flowering of Southern literature that has been dubbed a "renaissance" began soon after the publication of Mencken's intemperate essay.

American literature and for that matter Southern literature, as formal endeavors, began more than two centuries ago; Texas literature, for practical purposes, is barely a half-century old, dating from Dobie's first published writings in the 1920s. Though the following is far from a precise analogy, Texas literature today stands at approximately the same juncture as did American literature when Sydney Smith asked his ill-timed question, or as did Southern literature when Mencken launched his harangue. Perhaps Larry McMurtry is *our* Sydney Smith and H. L. Mencken rolled into one self-assured and beguilingly convincing critic. McMurtry has thrown down the gauntlet. "In the four quarters of the globe," he has asked in effect, "who reads a Texas book?" Who, that is, with even a shred of literary taste or self-respect. It remains to be seen whether circumstances will be as fortuitous for Texas litera-

ture in the near future as they were for American literature
following the gibes of people like Sydney Smith, or as they
were for Southern literature after Mencken's venomous gener-
alizations about Southern culture.

Time is required for a literary tradition to develop. Even
more time is needed for just appreciation and critical understanding of the tradition to evolve. The latter—critical appreciation and understanding—is really a public relations problem
that must be worked on slowly but relentlessly. Reviewers,
critics, and commentators have to be sold on the idea of a
literature's existence. That literature must be widely taught
over a long period of time in public-school and college class-
rooms. (Recall that it was well into the twentieth century before the first college-level course in American literature was
offered.) It seems to me that there are at least three stages
in the study and appreciation of any literature that must be
surmounted before the legitimacy of the literature is firmly es-
tablished. The first stage is simply recognition: it must be recognized that here is a body of literature worthy of serious
scrutiny and attention. The second stage is definition and description: boundaries must be drawn, and catalogues of relevant texts must be compiled. The third stage is critical judgment and discrimination: evaluations of authors and works
must be formulated, and the literature must be placed in a
comparative context with other literatures.

Texas writing has more or less successfully weathered
the first step; most readers, at least most Texas readers, are
probably willing to grant the existence of a body of works that
may be justifiably called "Texas literature." The status of
Texas writing with regard to the second stage is more prob-
lematical. The parameters that encompass Texas literature
have never been defined to everybody's satisfaction, and may
never be. A troublesome question, for example—and one that
grows more troublesome with every passing year—is, Who
are the Texas writers? (A similar question, incidentally, also

vexes the study of American literature: Were Aldous Huxley and W. H. Auden and Vladimir Nabokov *American* writers? Were Henry James and T. S. Eliot?) With regard to Texas literature there is no denying that J. Frank Dobie, Walter Prescott Webb, and Roy Bedichek—once worshipped as the "Holy Trinity of Texas Letters"—were Texas writers; they were born and bred in Texas, and they proudly boasted of their Texanness wherever two or three were gathered together to listen. Among today's authors no one would dispute the fact that John Graves and Elmer Kelton and Benjamin Capps are Texas writers.

But what about someone like Donald Barthelme? Barthelme was reared in Houston but lived in the East during most of his so far very successful career. He returned to Texas a short time back to teach creative writing at the University of Houston, but he has had little to say about the state in his published works; interestingly, though, he recently proclaimed "that taking the thing state by state, there are more good writers in Texas than anywhere in the country save New York and California." At any rate, despite McMurtry's lament earlier in this book that he had ever questioned Barthelme's "credentials as a Texan," it appears to me that doubts concerning those credentials have not yet been completely dissipated. On the other side of the coin, can authors such as Max Apple and Beverly Lowry and Laura Furman, who grew up in other regions but have spent much time in Texas of late, be labeled, with any justice, Texas writers? Or for that matter can a certain well-known man of American letters, who shall remain nameless but who lived in Texas for several years (and who still maintains a home in Austin) writing what he modestly called a "blockbuster" novel about the state—can he be called, or does he even care to be called, a Texas writer?

McMurtry, in "Ever a Bridegroom," takes a hard line in defining the Texas writer: ". . . only those born and raised in Texas," he asserts, "have the dubious honor of literary citizenship. Even writers who become absorbed in the state, and make good use of some part of it . . . shouldn't have to consider themselves Texas writers." The Texas Institute of Letters, on the other hand, takes a more liberal, not to say hopelessly diffusive, view of the question. The TIL seems intent on gathering into its fold any notable writer who crosses the Red River, whether by plane, train, or automobile. A measured definition of the Texas writer no doubt lies somewhere between these extremes. Certainly migration, and the immigrant who is the human figure in the phenomenon of migration, is as much a part of the Texas myth as it is of the larger American myth. Migrant writers, like migrant executives of high-tech electronics industries, must be granted the right to become naturalized Texas citizens, following an appropriate period of acculturation and assimilation, of course. Dues of citizenship must be paid. The question is, How high should the dues be set? I do not know the answer to that question, nor do I intend to explore it further here. The point is, as interest in Texas books grows, the inexorable homogenization of American—and Texan—society makes it more and more difficult to say who is and who is not a Texas writer.

In the scheme I outlined previously, the third stage in the study of a body of writing is sustained critical evaluation and appreciation, an activity that ultimately should yield a consensus as to the overall quality of the literature. The study of Texas literature has not yet reached this stage—or, if so, just barely. McMurtry's 1981 barrage from the pages of the *Texas Observer* ignited a firestorm of controversy as to the quality, or lack of quality, of Texas writing, in part, I think, because it violated the polite deference to each other's books that Texas writers and critics had tended over the years to maintain. Without question McMurtry hit a nerve. There were outraged reactions, heated commentary from every corner of Texas culture. The ensuing turmoil even caught the attention of the *New York Times* and the *Washington Post*; indeed it was considered important enough that in 1986, *Texas Monthly*'s Sesquicentennial "collector's issue," which bears the title "Texas, Our Texas: 150 Moments That Made Us The Way We Are," included an account of the verbal battle. Now that the dust has settled a bit, we discern a growing accumulation of criticism—mostly drifts from the departed sandstorm—but it seems clear that extant criticism of Texas writing is still relatively slight. I am not foolish enough to suggest that what I am about to say represents an incipient consensus judgment on Texas writing, but I want to make a few comments—perhaps most are fairly obvious—on the quality of Texas literature considered within the context of American literature generally.

First, I think it should be noted that Texas literature suffers from the limited generical range that its writers, to this point, have exhibited. Texas literature is essentially a literature of non-dramatic prose. Novelists, short-story writers, folklorists, historians, journalists, and practitioners of various kinds of expository prose have flourished within the state's borders throughout most of the twentieth century. Poets and playwrights have not. In 1981, in "Ever a Bridegroom," McMurtry could find only one Texas writer on whom he heaped unqualified praise: the poet Vassar Miller. Perhaps unfortunately, since Miller is without question an extremely talented poet, McMurtry's judgment has yet to be verified; Miller has so far failed to attract continuing regional, or national, critical acclaim. But even if McMurtry is correct in claiming that Miller is the cream of the contemporary crop of Texas writers, she remains the exception that proves the rule. In Texas, prose-writers—particularly novelists—still ride tall in the saddle.

Second, let it be admitted, right off, that there have been no literary geniuses to emerge from Texas. (I cannot define the term "literary genius," but I know one when I read one.)

A possible exception to this generalization is Katherine Anne Porter—if, that is, considering what I have said about the problem of definition, a case can be made for Porter's being branded a Texas writer, since she spent most of her literary life in voluntary and sometimes embittered exile from Texas. But maybe Porter is an exception, or a partial one—a potential genius, anyway, who wrote a handful of stunningly good stories, many of them set in Texas, that will be read as long as the English language and the printed word endure. Otherwise, I doubt that even the most optimistic Texas chauvinist would claim that the state has produced any truly great writers.

No, the brightest lights in the Texas literary galaxy rarely twinkle in the American literary heavens. Since his death in 1964 J. Frank Dobie—the founding father of Texas literature, for decades the state's cultural arbiter—has been pilloried by critics and blindsided by detractors. His literary reputation, once untarnished and impregnable, is now but a heap of rusted, abandoned scrap metal. Unquestionably Dobie's significance is largely historical rather than aesthetic. He was a literary pioneer who blazed a trail for later Texas writers to follow. But it is now plain to see, as it was not during his lifetime, that, to put it gently, he was not a great writer.

I venture to say that the most distinguished—as opposed to best-selling—living Texas writer is John Graves, who in a sense works within the ruralist tradition initiated by Dobie, Webb, and Bedichek. Graves is a professional, a writer who applies an exacting standard to his own performance. In my view he is the most skillful manipulator of language on the Texas literary scene today, a creator, as Joe Holley has said, of "forceful and eloquent prose." Future generations will find, I predict, Graves's wonderful meditation *Goodbye to a River* (1960)—despite, or perhaps because of, its ruralist bias—both pleasurable and profitable to read. But I think that Graves, who is modest about his literary accomplishment, would probably agree with my judgment that, alas, he is not a literary genius.

At the present time, of course, the Texas author who enjoys the greatest national popularity is the ubiquitous Larry
McMurtry. (Attempting to prevent McMurtry's name from
popping up too frequently in an essay such as this one is like
trying to stamp out the toadstools after a week of heavy rains.)
McMurtry is a very inventive and prolific writer, and his winning a Pulitzer Prize for fiction for *Lonesome Dove* (1985) was a
well-deserved honor. Texans are justifiably proud that a native
son has "made it" as a nationally, even internationally, ac-
claimed writer, but McMurtry's standing with posterity is an
issue that is far from settled. He has published a great deal—
perhaps too much—and I fear that his aggregate fictional output may contain more dross than nuggets of precious metal.

In spite of the tendency of literate Texans, then, to over-
rate their Dobies and Graveses and McMurtrys, Texas is not,
on the other hand, the vast cultural wasteland that some have
portrayed it to be. We have dozens of good, interesting, competent, and even undervalued writers who have practiced their
craft with integrity and diligence during the last half-century
or so. From East Texas, we have the three Williams—William
Humphrey, William Owens, and William Goyen—who have
yet to receive the regional, much less national, recognition
they deserve. From West Texas, Elmer Kelton, Benjamin
Capps, and Robert Flynn are excellent novelists who are often
ignored by reviewers and critics. (In his survey, for example,
McMurtry directs one disparaging comment toward Flynn,
mentions Capps in passing, and slights Kelton altogether;
only one book by the three, Capps's *A Woman of the People,*
shows up on Greene's "fifty best" list.) From South Texas,
Rolando Hinojosa and the late Tomás Rivera have given im-
petus in recent years to a vital and vibrant Texas Mexican
literature that grows in strength and stature year by year.
We have even witnessed, as Texas becomes ever more citified,
the appearance of a few works about urban life in the state
that are worthy of critical attention. I am thinking of books

such as Billy Lee Brammer's *The Gay Place* (1961), or of two
Dallas novels, Edwin Shrake's *Strange Peaches* (1972) and
Bryan Woolley's *November 22* (1981), or of Laura Furman's
The Shadow Line (1982) and David Lindsey's *A Cold Mind*
(1983) and *Heat from Another Sun* (1984), novels that owe much
of their narrative force to their Houston settings.

I allude, one more time, to McMurtry's conclusion that
Texas literature is a "failure." I, in fact, concur with McMurtry's judgment that Texas literature, within the context of the
American literary tradition, is on the whole insular, ingrown,
and inferior. I do not agree that Texas literature is therefore a
failed literature. I prefer to think of it as a developing literature. (If there is such a thing as a "developing economy," then
I suppose there can also be a developing literature.) To reiter-
ate, Texas literature is still young, still growing. I will not predict that Texas writing is about to blossom, the way American
writing blossomed in the middle decades of the previous century. Given the lessons of history, though, I would not be surprised if it did.

To end with what seems an appropriate comparison,
since we are talking about *Texas* literature, I invoke the analogy of a nineteenth-century trail drive, which proceeded a leg
at a time, confronting and surmounting obstacles, until the
promised land of the railhead at the end of the long trail was
reached. Texas literature has overcome a number of obstacles
already, but the question is, How close are we to Dodge? Are
the bright lights in view, or are there still many rivers to cross,
many stampedes and rainstorms and dust storms yet to be en-
dured before trail's end—and the bars and casinos and the
pleasures of the flesh—are attained? Is Texas writing on the
margins of a breakthrough, a triumphant culmination? We
shall see.

A positive sign that such a culmination may very well be

in the offing is that Texas, as a cultural entity, possesses the sustaining mythology, the sense of group identity, the self-consciousness and determination that seem to form the necessary support system for the emergence of a significant "national" literature. If any state or region in America is able to withstand in years to come the growing pressures of standardization and homogenization, it ought to be Texas. All of the rapid and sweeping changes the state is currently undergoing, even the recent economic downturn—these, as T. R. Fehren-bach has claimed, may ultimately prove illusory, at least as far as their effect on the Texas mythos is concerned. Even as Texas becomes overwhelmingly urban and its population is transformed by the influx of people from other states and regions, the Texas myth lives on. "Midnight cowboys" and "urban cowboys" replace real cowboys, but in one form or another the myth of the cowboy survives.

And the myth provides a powerful stimulus to literary activity in the state—indeed to artistic activity of all kinds. It supplies, as McMurtry's *Lonesome Dove* memorably illustrates, a rich texture of tradition, a frame of reference, within which the artist may work. Given these hopeful conditions, we have now, I suppose, only to await the arrival of a Texas literary genius. But genius, of whatever stripe, seems to be an accident of birth, as unpredictable in its origin as it is difficult to recognize and to nurture. Maybe there is a literary genius—a Texas Whitman or Faulkner—out there right now, growing up in Muleshoe or Decatur or Jasper, or beginning to struggle with his or her craft in Houston or Dallas or Austin. Then again, maybe there is not. (Some developing economies develop; others do not. Why should developing literatures be any different?) But Texans are nothing if not optimistic. Texas literature, like Texas history, still seems, to Texans, an unfinished saga. Texas literature, we confidently predict, has its best days ahead of it. The only thing that appears certain, there-fore—and the only forecast I am bold enough to make—is that Texas's literary future will be interesting and pleasantly surprising.

SELECTED BIBLIOGRAPHY

The following is a list of works that offer bibliographical and interpretive assistance to readers who wish to look further into the subject of Texas writing. The listing is far from exhaustive; it is intended merely to suggest some places to begin.

Anderson, John Q., Edwin W. Gaston, and James W. Lee, eds. *Southwestern American Literature: A Bibliography.* Chicago: Swallow Press, 1980.
The Southwest is here defined as Oklahoma, Texas, New Mexico, and Arizona. The bibliography is current only through the mid-1970s, but contains helpful listings for individual authors as well as for a variety of subject areas.

Bennett, Patrick. *Talking with Texas Writers: Twelve Interviews.* College Station: Texas A&M University Press, 1980.
Generally illuminating interviews with Larry McMurtry, John Graves, Elmer Kelton, A. C. Greene, Shelby Hearon, William Goyen, and a half-dozen other Texas writers. Contains bibliographies of the publications (to 1980) of each of the interviewees.

Clifford, Craig Edward. *In the Deep Heart's Core: Reflections on Life, Letters, and Texas.* College Station: Texas A&M University Press, 1985.

A collection of essays by an expatriate Texan recently returned to the state. Texas writers and their writings loom large in the author's reflections on his native terrain. Contains "A Personal Bibliography."

Dobie, J. Frank. *Guide to Life and Literature of the Southwest.* Revised Edition. Dallas: Southern Methodist University Press, 1952.
Classic annotated bibliography, developed as a supplement to Dobie's legendary Southwestern literature course at the University of Texas at Austin. Defines the Southwest vaguely: the region from West Texas to Southern California, plus "anything else north, south, east, or west that anybody wants to bring in." Still quite readable. Strong on history and memoirs. On the other hand, the work is now badly out of date, and it is weak on fiction, the genre in which most Texas writers have excelled.

Graham, Don. *Texas: A Literary Portrait.* San Antonio: Corona Publishing, 1985.
Three books in one: a portfolio of photographs by Nell Blakely, a gathering of brief comments on Texas by a variety of writers (mostly outlanders), and Don Graham's informal and entertaining discussion of the literature that has emerged from the different areas of the state. Contains a bibliography.

Graham, Don, James W. Lee, and William T. Pilkington, eds. *The Texas Literary Tradition: Fiction, Folklore, History.* Austin: College of Liberal Arts of the University of Texas and the Texas State Historical Association, 1983.
A collection of essays on various aspects of Texas literature. This volume was an outgrowth of the 1983 Texas Literary Tradition symposium, held at the University of Texas at Austin. Some of the pieces included are versions of papers read at

the conference; others were written especially for the book. Contains an extensive annotated bibliography.

Greene, A. C. *The Fifty Best Books on Texas*. Dallas: Pressworks Publishing, 1982.
An expanded version of Greene's *Texas Monthly* article, "The Fifty Best Texas Books." The book features a useful introduction not found in the article.

Heinemann, Alison, ed. *Threads of Texas Literature: A Multi-Cultural Design*. Austin: Texas Circuit, 1980.
Pamphlet published in conjunction with a conference on "contemporary Texas literature," convened in Austin in March 1980. Includes essays on current Anglo writing in Texas, black and Chicano writing in the state, Texas women writers, and small-press publishing.

Lee, James Ward. *Classics of Texas Fiction*. Dallas: E-Heart Press, 1987.
Short "reviews," written in 1986 for the Sesquicentennial celebration, of forty-seven "classic" works of Texas fiction. Lee also offers a catalogue of seventy-one additional worthwhile Texas novels, each briefly annotated, and a year-by-year list, beginning in 1941, of the Texas Institute of Letters's award-winning novels.

McMurtry, Larry. *In a Narrow Grave: Essays on Texas*. Albuquerque: University of New Mexico Press, 1983. (Originally published by Encino Press, Austin, in 1968.)
Witty, lucid essays on Texas culture. McMurtry's initial assault on Texas literature was launched in one of the pieces, "Southwestern Literature?" In it, he stormed the citadel of the Dobie-Webb-Bedichek fortress. Contains an interesting, though extremely eccentric, bibliography.

Major, Mabel, and T. M. Pearce. *Southwest Heritage: A Literary History with Bibliographies.* Third Edition. Albuquerque: University of New Mexico Press, 1972.
Defines the Southwest as Arkansas, Oklahoma, Texas, New Mexico, and Arizona. Very helpful reference tool. Particularly good at providing material on the beginnings of Texas and Southwestern literature. As the subtitle indicates, contains extensive bibliographies.

O'Connor, Robert F., ed. *Texas Myths.* College Station: Texas A&M University Press, 1986.
A volume of essays commissioned by the Texas Committee for the Humanities. Though none of them deals directly with the state's writing, as a group they supply essential information concerning the mythological backgrounds of Texas literature and culture.

Pilkington, William T. *Imagining Texas: The Literature of the Lone Star State.* Boston: American Press, 1981.
Succinct descriptive survey of Texas literature, which is said to have been "a going concern only since the 1920s." Contains a brief bibliographical essay.

NOTES ON CONTRIBUTORS

CRAIG CLIFFORD grew up outside Houston, Texas. He holds a Ph.D. in philosophy from the State University of New York at Buffalo and now teaches philosophy and is University Scholar at Tarleton State University in Stephenville, Texas. Clifford is the author of *In the Deep Heart's Core: Reflections on Life, Letters, and Texas* (1985) and has completed a second book, *Learned Ignorance in the Medicine Bow Mountains,* a critique of what he calls "pseudo-intellectual prejudice."

Born in rural Collin County, Texas, DON GRAHAM grew up in Dallas. He has taught at the University of Pennsylvania and is currently J. Frank Dobie Regents Professor of English and American Literature at the University of Texas at Austin. Graham is coeditor (with James W. Lee and Tom Pilkington) of *The Texas Literary Tradition: Fiction, Folklore, History* (1983), editor of *South by Southwest: 24 Stories from Modern Texas* (1986), and author of *Cowboys and Cadillacs: How Hollywood Looks at Texas* (1983) and *Texas: A Literary Portrait* (1985). His *No Name on the Bullet: A Biography of Audie Murphy* will be published by Viking in 1989.

A native of Abilene, Texas, A. C. GREENE has long been recognized as the sage of Dallas. He is a columnist for the *Dallas
Morning News,* essayist for PBS's "MacNeil/Lehrer Newshour,"
and author of several books on his adopted city. Greene's most
highly praised work to date is *A Personal Country* (1969), a collection of ruminations on West Texas.

JAMES WARD LEE, born and reared in Alabama, has taught
and written on Texas and Southwestern literature for a quarter-
century. He was general editor of the Southwest Writers pamphlet series published by Steck-Vaughn in the late 1960s. He
has been a longtime active member and has served as president of the Texas Folklore Society. He is the author of *Classics
of Texas Fiction* (1987). Currently Lee is chair of the English
Department and director of the Center for Texas Studies at the
University of North Texas in Denton.

Born in Laredo, Texas, JOSÉ E. LIMÓN is chair and associate
professor of American Studies at the University of California
at Santa Cruz. He has published several articles on Chicano
literature and is author of a study of society and folklore in
Mexican American South Texas to be published by the University of Wisconsin Press.

Born in Wichita Falls, Texas, LARRY McMURTRY grew up
on his family's ranch near Archer City. Ever since the publication of his first novel, *Horseman, Pass By* (1961), McMurtry has
been a well-known American writer, as well as a dealer in rare
books. During his career he has lived in Fort Worth, Houston,
Washington, D.C., and currently, having come full circle, once
again calls Archer City home. McMurtry's trail-drive novel,
Lonesome Dove (1985), won a Pulitzer Prize for fiction. His
most recently published novel is *Anything for Billy* (1988).

CELIA MORRIS was born in Houston, Texas. She attended the University of Texas at Austin and has lived for extended periods in Austin and in New York City. She currently resides in Washington, D.C. She is author of the award-winning biography *Fanny Wright: Rebel in America* (1984; under the name Celia Morris Eckhardt). At present she is writing a political novel set in Texas.

Born in Fort Worth, Texas, and reared on a farm south of that city, TOM PILKINGTON is professor of English at Tarleton State University in Stephenville, Texas. He is one of the general editors of *A Literary History of the American West* (1987). Pilkington has published numerous books and articles on Southwestern and Texas literature, including *My Blood's Country: Studies in Southwestern Literature* (1973) and *Imagining Texas: The Literature of the Lone Star State* (1981).

A native of Quanah in northwest Texas, CLAY REYNOLDS is novelist-in-residence at the University of North Texas. Reynolds is the author of two novels, *The Vigil* and *Agatite,* both published in 1986, and a third, *Franklin's Crossing,* which will appear in 1989. He has also published a scholarly study, *Stage Left: The Development of the American Social Drama in the Thirties* (1986).

Born in Ohio, MARSHALL TERRY has lived in Dallas, Texas, for three decades. He is professor of English and director of the Creative Writing Program at Southern Methodist University and is the author of three novels— *Old Liberty* (1961), *Tom Northway* (1968), and *Ringer* (1987)—and a collection of short stories, *Dallas Stories* (1987). Terry is widely known for his leadership in promoting the work of the Texas Institute of Letters.

INDEX